National Bestseller Series

GETTING YA THROUGH THE SUMMER

Cooking for the Rushed

Getting Ya Through The Summer is all about healthy eating during the workweek while keeping the heat out of the house. Symbols make it clear how you will be cooking your meal to adjust for the heat of the day. It is the second book in the Cooking for the Rushed series and contains all the key components which made Life's on Fire a national bestseller.

This book focuses on meal plans. It teaches you to eat forwards instead of backwards so you are balancing your diet in the day. It teaches you how to create your own reusable grocery lists using recipes you now make. You will reduce your stress related to getting a healthy supper on the table and will save money on grocery and entertaining costs.

Cooking for the Rushed books are visual. A colored clock is situated at the top right hand corner of the book so that as a person flips through the recipes they can immediately know the preparation and how-long-before-we-eat times. Nutritional data is included directly to the left of the clocks. By looking at your supper recipe at the beginning of the day you will know how to adjust your fat intake and diet during the day. Recipes have color photos (no food styling tricks used) so you know exactly the way it looks when you prepare it. Symbols identify meal components for ease of substitution.

There are easy to follow instructions next to each ingredient. Detailed equipment lists for every meal are listed. The books have nutritionally balanced weeks of 5 suppers, including completed grocery lists for each week. Meals were extensively tested with real families on the go.

by Sandi Richard

Illustrated by Lorna Bennett

GETTING YA THROUGH THE SUMMER™
LIFE'S ON FIRE™
COOKING FOR THE RUSHED™
are trademarks of Cooking for the Rushed Inc.

All inquiries should be addressed to:

Cooking for the Rushed Inc.
P.O. Box 2056
Cochrane, Alberta
Canada T4C 1B8
E-Mail: rsrichard@cookingfortherushed.com
Web page: www.cookingfortherushed.com

National Library of Canada Cataloguing in Publication Data

Richard, Sandi, 1959-
   Getting ya through the summer

(Cooking for the rushed)
Includes index.
ISBN 0-9685226-1-0

   1. Quick and easy cookery. 2. Low-fat diet--Recipes.
I. Bennett, Lorna, 1960- II. Title. III. Series: Richard, Sandi,
1959- . Cooking for the rushed.

TX833.5.R52 2001   641.5'55   C2001-900340-4

Separations and film by Elite Lithographers Co. Ltd., Edmonton, AB
Printed in Canada by Friesens Corp., Altona, MB

10 9 8 7 6 5 4 3 2

Recipe analysis calculated using FOOD QUEST© (copyright of Jbw Associates Inc.); Canada's leading software designed to assist people with diabetes in managing their day to day food requirements and menu planning. This program is published in co-operation with the Canadian Diabetes Association. Neither party is responsible for the computation of the data found in this book.

To our reader with diabetes
"Getting Ya Through the Summer - Cooking for the Rushed" is not a cookbook which claims to cater to the complex dietary needs of a person with diabetes. The nature of this book is speed and nutrition. A large number of people have some form of diabetes therefore we feel it is necessary to provide information, on food choice values, that is as accurate as possible.

In view of the complex nature of health in relation to food, this book is not intended to replace professional or medical advice. The authors and publisher expressly disclaim any responsibility for any liability, loss, or risk, personal or otherwise, which is incurred as a consequence, directly or indirectly, of the use and application of any of the contents of this book.

If You Are Willing To Use

Your **BBQ** is not just a griller…it's your summer oven! Just think, it can keep your home cooler for 6 months of the year or more. Soooo if you have an old one it might be time for a new one. If a new BBQ is in your plans…we suggest; two inside burners with separate controls as well as a side burner for pots, a high lid with an upper rack and a temperature gauge.

A **crockpot** is not just a winter appliance…in fact it will save your butt when it gets too hot! It keeps your home cool and cooks while you're at work. You won't want to use this every night …but once a week you will love our "I cook, you clean" method of using it!

A **foil diffuser** is made by folding a long piece of heavy foil in half, shiny side out. The edges are crumpled together on all sides. The final size must be larger than the bottom of the pan you are using. When using your BBQ as an oven, the diffuser deflects the direct heat from the burners to prevent scorching the food in the bottom of the pan.

Foil wraps are amazing for reducing clean-up and for keeping the heat out of your home. We make our own so we can adjust the size of the wrap to the amount of food. Use wraps for cooking veggies, to stir-fry and for just about anything else in a BBQ. When doing a stir-fry, wrap twice with the second seam on the opposite side of the first seam. This way you avoid leaking…turn and check often.

Dedication

Once again I dedicate this book to my best friend, my husband Ron.
We have now worked side by side for five years…we have laughed
and cried and talked about nothing but food, sometimes for days at a
time! Not too many people can claim as I can, that their husband is
the most fun person in the world to work with!
I love you sooo much. Thanks for always enjoying a good challenge!

Also to our amazing children. None of us had any idea how much
our family would be exposed to the media this year! You have forged
through it like troopers!
Thanks for knowing how important this topic is to me!
Thank you for giving me the freedom to follow my dreams as well!
Most of all thank you for loving me!
I would have handpicked every one of you all over again!
I love you all sooo much!

Table of Contents

Food Fads Don't Work

(I know, I was addicted to them!)

Let Me Paint You A Picture

When this journey began for me 17 years ago after my second child, I was addicted to "different ways of eating" books! You know the ones...they're very trendy, and every second friend you know is telling you about the amazing results! Before you know it, you're looking in the mirror thoroughly disgusted with yourself for one reason or another. As if by osmosis, you buy the book...........

You tell me if you can relate to the next page!

A Diet of Stress

Week 1... Your emotion driven state of elation about **changing your life**, gets you going into **full force**. The preparation of the food and refiguring out how to eat may be hard, but before you know it the book you bought is keeping all it's promises.

Week 2... You have **more energy** and you feel fantastic. You are now a **walking advocate** and you're telling all your friends about the amazing results! You feel a new inner power and regained self-esteem.

Week 3... The kids baseball and dancing schedule are a little heavier than normal and the food schedule **begins to clash** with the home schedule. Kids are getting drive through meals or chicken fingers on a cookie sheet, but you're pretty much **hanging in there**. You've **only cheated twice** and you had a darn good reason!

Week 4... You don't want to admit to your friends that your **partner and kids are fed up** with the weird food, and that you are beginning to buckle with the **stress** of pulling off two types of meals (one for the family and one for you). It becomes **more than you can handle**. You become **discouraged and angry** with yourself and begin to blame outside forces. Slowly you stop drinking as much water as when you got started and begin to make time restraint excuses for turfing the exercise.

Week 5... Your friends and you start admitting that this **wasn't as easy as it looked** and have a good laugh at how you thought you could pull off this excruciating way of eating. Although you laugh on the outside, you feel empty and hurt inside. You wonder what's wrong with you. You **feel depressed** and the next thing you tell yourself is, "Why not have the chocolate bar...after all **it's hopeless**!"

This is exactly how I felt until I realized that...

**like 85% of North Americans,
I was simply eating backwards!**

That's when things changed!

What the Heck Does Eating Forwards Mean?

Well, let me explain!

If you know you are having cheesy lasagna for supper, and you know this at the beginning of the day, will you feel like a heavy pasta or cheese dish at lunch? Not likely!

Natural weight control and balanced moods can really be this easy! Our lives are out of control…soooo our eating is out of control!

Eating forwards is a simple way for the average person to balance what they are eating in the day.

I am having an extremely low-fat supper tonight. I know I have the groceries in the house because I have a meal plan and I went and bought the groceries for the week (see page 96 to learn how easy this is). I glance at the recipe and notice there is pasta served with the meal and there is brown sugar in the sauce. My brain says I can have a higher fat lunch today, take it easy on the carbs, and watch my sugar intake!

…ooor I glance at my recipe and see I am having a mealtime salad, which is higher in fat, low on carbs and savory rather than sweet. I can allow myself carbs at lunch and a little sugar won't hurt.

9

Eating Forwards (Cont.)

When I wrote <u>Life's on Fire - Cooking for the Rushed</u> I tried to downplay the meal planning aspect of the book. Why? I was afraid people would break into a cold sweat with yet another person trying to over-organize their already over-scheduled lives. I was afraid that people would look past the simplicity of what I wanted so badly to explain!

Eating Should Be Normal, Not Complicated!!!

...sooo, I focused on three key points instead.

✔ 1. Food must be "to die for" delicious

✔ 2. Food must be fast (because we have stressful schedules)

✔ 3. Food must be easily purchased at a grocery store
   ...or you will fall off the health wagon!

We tested the recipes pumping out up to 160 meals a week for 5 1/2 years for three books. Why would we go to all that trouble? Our goal was to teach people to eat forwards and to meal plan forwards. If the recipes were fantastic and easy enough for even a noncook…people would trust the grocery lists. They would then begin to understand how meal planning would not only improve their health, but reduce stress in their homes while saving them money on groceries!

I had no idea how many people would understand the value of those grocery lists right off the bat! Families across the nation are meal planning and it is changing their health. Grocery bills are plummeting, partners who never cooked before are cooking, people are feeling less stress and people who had struggled with food issues are losing weight or feeling their moods are more balanced!

We've heard from thousands of these families. People have e-mailed us, written us letters, called in to talk shows, and gone out of their way to come and tell us their stories at bookstores and cooking events. WOW!!!

We're often asked the question, "Why don't you talk more about the system you've developed? Now that we know people trust our recipes and are willing to make a few changes it will be our mission this year to get people meal planning.

For those of you who have already made the decision to improve your eating life, my hat is off to all of you!!

Understanding The Media
and Celebrity Eating

...and How It Screws Us Up!!

L. BENNETT

We are so media driven. If we are not watching T.V. we are listening to the radio, reading newspapers or magazines...you name it! We somehow respect celebrities like they are our extended families ...and we're proud that they made it to the top. We listen to them, we admire them, and we want to be like them in one way or another. We overlook the fact that many are on mood enhancing drugs to cope, their marriages regularly fall apart and <u>their job is to stay slim, look beautiful and smile</u>! The scary thing we mostly overlook is that many of them have a nanny, a cook, a housekeeper and possibly even a trainer. To pull off what they do, they need to, but then we need to recognize <u>their opinions are no longer for the average person</u>...aaaand it's average people who are listening!

We are being sent confusing messages about food all the time.

While our favorite celebrities flash by the screen, high fat, chemical laced, sodium pumped food in packages, on TV commercials, flash by the screen directly before or after them!!! To make it worse, celebrities advocate their food opinions to the average world even though the circumstances around their lifestyle are not average. North Americans somehow miss this! I'll never forget the phase where so many celebrities claimed, "...every animal in the animal kingdom has been weaned off their mother's breast at 6 weeks. We don't need milk!" Don't people in the public eye understand that this is an elitist point of view?

11

The impact of the previous statement may have just turned 10,000 teens over to soda pop. People in the public eye don't honestly think the parents in these homes are saying things like, "Oh really Johnny, you've decided to stop drinking milk, then let me run out and buy you some slow release calcium supplements!!!" …Ooooor, "Johnny…let's completely alter our diet and look for calcium-enriched foods!!!" If you want to know the real impact of that statement, just ask some doctors about the high rates of childhood osteoporosis they're seeing these days!

We are in an era of "Getting Real", yet with food we're living a fantasy.

We Have Made Food Too Hard and Too Easy, That's What's REAL!!!

We are being sent mixed messages all the time. On the one hand, new books with complicated formulas for eating are thrown in our face every time we turn around. On the other hand, TV commercials try to legitimize unhealthy heat and serve suppers as a solution for reducing stress in our homes. What hope have we got when we walk by samples of these same foods while grocery shopping. As our heads are reeling over our work and home schedules, all we remember are the TV commercials showing put-together parents feeding their calm happy children the food they like.

Voila…a recipe all right…a recipe for disaster!

Have you noticed the new renovations in the grocery stores lately? Stores are making space to accommodate the increasing demand for supper-in-a-box type foods. They're not spending all that money in the hope that we will purchase these products. Not only are we buying this stuff - We are demanding it!!

I am often asked, when in the media or speaking at conferences, if I believe dealing with inner emotions or childhood experiences are a big part of our food problems. I think this can be part of it, but I mostly think we need to uncomplicate the food information highway in our homes.

A Different Way
of Thinking
= SPEED

...and healthy eating in the summer

For your benefit we repeated a few key components of the system developed in <u>Life's on Fire - Cooking for the Rushed</u>. If you need more details about the system refer to <u>Life's on Fire</u>. Also visit our website.

www.cookingfortherushed.com

My Food Beliefs

If nutritious food can't be fast, you may eat something you shouldn't.

Calories from fat should not exceed **30%** of your total caloric intake on a **daily** basis.

Frozen vegetables may be healthier than fresh! Wow, that's a big one!! Food manufacturers have the capability to remove some of the harmful chemicals off vegetables by washing, in a much more advanced way than we can in our home. Think about it!! There's a time to use fresh, when you have time to remove the chemicals properly. Let someone else do the work when you're in a rush.

Meats should be **trimmed**, so purchase them that way. You don't have time. Boneless, skinless chicken is best! Don't tell yourself you can't afford it, tell yourself you need that help for cooking quickly. Besides, are you really saving money when buying untrimmed or cheaper cuts? When I buy a 750 g pkg of untrimmed steak, I end up with 500 g and worse, it takes me extra time I don't have!

Carbohydrates are **essential** for energy. Dry pasta, rice and potatoes are great for storage and have a high rate of success. Use different varieties of pasta and rice to make meals more interesting. Choose whole grain whenever possible. It's okay to buy dehydrated potato flakes, canned potatoes or dehydrated potato slices. If you don't consider speed, what's the alternative?

If you have kids, remember, **you are not running a restaurant**. You need to provide them with a protein, a carbohydrate and a fruit or vegetable at supper. Some will be meat eaters and some will be vegetarians. Most will like the carbohydrate. Make a rule that they **must** have a very small **taste** of the part they hate. Don't make them gag, just introduce it. Suggest they down it with milk, plug their nose, or do whatever it takes. This introduces different flavors into their palate and eventually eliminates stress for you! Also don't let them snack if they don't eat the part they usually like. This is your stamp of approval for poor eating habits!!

Do You Shoulder the Burden of Getting Supper On the Table?

...you may be part of the problem!

Share Your Information

    If you are the cook of the house and tired of not getting help, but you don't share your information...you may be part of the problem!

    Ouch!!! I know, I've had more people give me the glare of death when I say that...but those same people tend to be the ones who later go out of their way to let me know their eating lives have changed!

Share Your Information

Here's an easy analogy…My husband, Ron, mulls over financial computer programs for our company. He's always interested in new information. He installs the software, learns the programs and is in touch with the help desk while figuring everything out! Our business runs smooth because Ron takes care of those very important things!

When Ron has to leave for a few days and I need to input information into the system…I break into a cold sweat. Why?

- I fear I am going to screw up (and is he going to spend the next week trying to find my error).
- I'm tackling something that is going to take me three times as long, that I'm not going to do half as well.

Can you see how this relates to the noncook? They may feel insecure about screwing up a job that you already do well.

Going back to the computer story...Ron and I came up with a solution. Ron leaves me a sheet with the information I need. This way, I don't screw up all his work and he doesn't feel like every time he's away he has to play catch up. The funny part is, I feel much more independent and better about myself every time I know how to input the accounting!

I have never met one adult who says,
"I'M JUST LIVING TO BE DEPENDANT ON ANOTHER HUMAN BEING."
Sometimes a person just needs to know where to start!

COOKING IS A FORM OF INDEPENDENCE

If 85% of North Americans have no idea what they are having for supper until supper, chances are you are in this group. When the noncook knows where to start and feels like they can pull off a healthy supper without help, they are much more likely to take on the job.

...sooo, share your information!!!

This will change the dynamics of supper in your home!!!

16

One Step at a Time

When I speak about sharing your information at conferences, people often respond defensively and say…

"How come you're telling me I still have to do all the thinking <u>and</u> pull the meal plan together in order for this to work? I want someone else to do the thinking for a change."

My answer is simple…If you want things to change and you have always been the one to do and plan everything…you will need to get your family involved gradually! However, if you think your family instinctively will know how to help, when you've always handled it before, you can continue to feel sorry for yourself and stay right where you are!

…oooor…

You have followed all the instructions on how to do your meal plans and grocery lists stress free from page 96…so you know the groceries are in the house.

Step 1

Choose a recipe according to what is happening in your life the following evening.

Step 2

You are making a recipe from another book and the recipe doesn't include an equipment list…jot down your own equipment list. Write it on the recipe or on a piece of note paper attached to the recipe.

Step 3

Place the recipe beside the stove the night before, making sure everyone in the family knows what you are having for supper the following night. Ask one member (nicely) to take out all the equipment and any nonrefrigerated ingredients when they get home the following day. Have them place everything beside the stove, so you are ready to begin when you arrive home! Suggest that if they have time to get it started, great…but if they don't…just that part will make you feel like you're not alone!

Watch what starts to happen!!!

Different Colors - WHY?

RED		YELLOW

and

Less Cutting and Chopping   More Cutting and Chopping

Eating time is **30 minutes**
... when you need to get your butt out of the house fast.

**If either Red or Yellow have Wings,
eating time is 25 minutes**

GREEN		BLUE

and

Less Cutting and Chopping   More Cutting and Chopping

Eating time is **60 minutes**.
...when you have a small window of opportunity to prepare,
but need to rush off somewhere or you want to relax before you eat.

How the symbols on the left of the recipe work

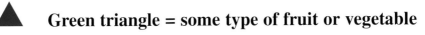 Red circle = some type of protein

Blue square = some type of carbohydrate

Green triangle = some type of fruit or vegetable

We are not accustomed to reading a recipe that gives you all the components of a meal. It's usually only one component. These symbols help you breeze through each step with a clear indication of which part of the meal you are working on.

Families like these symbols for another reason!
When a person is miraculously free on the weekend for a while (which is clearly some strange phenomenon), they sickeningly choose to freeze ahead some meals in their spare time. (They are only my friends, I'm not related!)
They choose their favorite freezer type meals, make up their own grocery list and follow the main course symbols only. Then when they pull them out during the week they follow the recipe to fill in the missing components. (eg. salad, pasta, etc...)

The symbols are very useful for <u>adults</u> who have adopted a belief in food research, but need to provide their children with a balanced diet until they are old enough to apply their own beliefs.

Make the whole meal, however:
• If you believe in eating mostly meats with fruits and vegetables:
  Serve yourself the red circle and the green triangle.
• If you believe you should combine a vegetable with a meat or a carbohydrate but not both:
  Serve yourself the green triangle with one of the others.
• If you believe that meat is not good for your body:
  Serve yourself the blue square with the green triangle. (This doesn't however always make for a very interesting vegetarian meal, but it will help in a rush.)

For rushed individuals <u>without</u> children.
Do whatever your little heart desires and you can use the symbols to cater to your own beliefs.

 Note: If you are vegetarian, the celery huggers displayed on each week's intro page indicate a great meal with tofu, plain veggies, nuts, seeds, or soya replacement for ground beef.

Rethinking Summer Eating!!!

The weather starts to get warm and all of a sudden everyone, at the same time, decides that exercise is going to be their #1 goal in life! After all, everything is new in the spring. The birds are chirping, the flowers are blooming and the hope of a brand new day is fresh in the air. We want to be outdoors, close to nature! People are walking, the streets come alive and you can smell a BBQ grilling it's wonders around every corner!

Within three weeks you get a little tired of BBQ chicken, BBQ steak, BBQ hamburgers, BBQ hotdogs and you really don't care if you see another BBQ'd anything for a while!

It's now summer and definitely too hot to cook in the house…so you start the next phase, which is salads and fruit or veggies with dip! That'll last about three days! Drive-thru becomes a natural…oh, what the heck, who wants to cook in this heat!!!

North Americans eat out and take-out more in the hot weather than they do when it's cold. Sooooo the ironic part of this is while we are possibly getting more exercise than we have all year, we are ingesting more fat and garbage calories than we have all year!

When I noticed I did this myself (I can't tell you how many times tacos with salsa was supper), I started to rethink the use of two appliances. When it came time to test the recipes for this book, I chose a BBQ that the average person could afford to purchase and a crockpot with a removable center pot. You will find these are two of the best investments you can make for the health of your family in the summer. Your BBQ is not just for grilling, it's your warm weather oven!

Do you realize that if you live in a location with four seasons you can probably use your BBQ, without climbing through snow, for at least 6 months of the year. That's half the year…and yet we generally see outdoor cooking as a short season!

You'll notice we've done some other things a little differently as well…all in the attempt to keep the heat out of the house and eat great tasting food that's actually good for you!

Just like in our book <u>Life's on Fire</u> we will ask you to try and bend your head around doing things a little differently than you may be used to! If you do, you will notice a drastic **decrease in stress**, your **grocery bills will drop** and **summer cooking** will be something that **you will look forward to**!

We Added Some Symbols
Beneath The Time Clocks

Here's what they mean

 BBQ (preheated)
as an oven

 BBQ grill

 "I cook, you clean night" (This means while one family member is doing the dishes another is taking care of a very fast prep for the following evening.)
This meal is generally done in a crockpot, stored in the fridge overnight and plugged in the next morning...not always so check your recipe the night before.

 Precooked meat is used to prepare a quick meal. (Ready-to-eat roasting chickens can be purchased from most delis and large grocery stores.)

 This meal is for one of those days when it's not too hot and you can throw together a very quick stir-fry.

Note: Sometimes we may use two appliances. Eg; Beef Barley Soup is an "I cook, you clean meal"….however when you get in the door you preheat the BBQ and stir together ingredients for corn muffins. These will be baked in your preheated BBQ. In a case like this we always choose the symbol which represents the greater part of the meal.

Cutting for Speed

No fancy schmancy in the work week

How to cut an onion

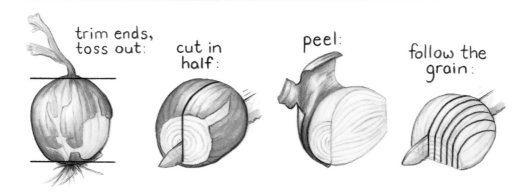

trim ends, toss out:

cut in half:

peel:

follow the grain:

How to cut a mushroom

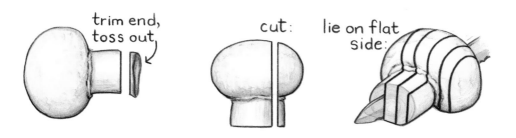

trim end, toss out,

cut:

lie on flat side:

How to prepare asparagus

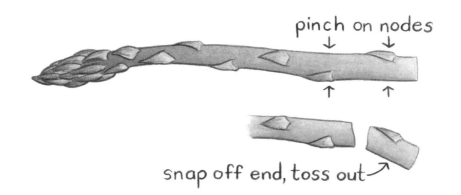

pinch on nodes

snap off end, toss out

How to cut peppers

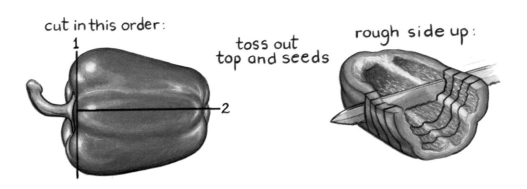

cut in this order:

1

2

toss out
top and seeds

rough side up:

How to cut green onion

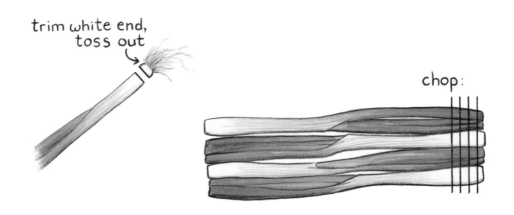

trim white end,
toss out

chop:

Chicken breasts are sold in two different ways

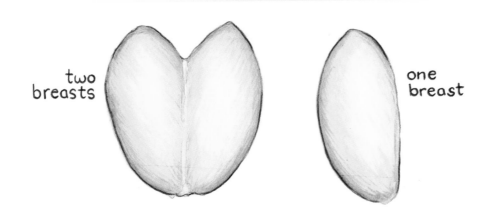

two
breasts

one
breast

You Must Own

Cutting Board

Make sure you have a good cutting board that doesn't slip and is easy to pick up. Remember, it's to dump the stuff you're cutting into the pan. I call it my easy food transferer. It's a bonus that it protects my counters.

Sharp Knives

We all would love to be able to afford sharp knives of great quality. I slowly purchased mine one at a time and gulped when I paid the price. A temporary fix can be to buy knives that have sharpening holders. If you have dull meat and vegetable knives, it's one more excuse to give up, and **we all know, we're looking for any excuse we can get!**

Large Microwave-Safe Pot for Rice

Sometimes rice should be cooked on the stove, sometimes in the microwave and sometimes in the oven. It's all a matter of low stress and timing!

Salad Spinner

They are only a few bucks. Watch for a deal, it's an invaluable time saving investment.

Apron

If you don't have one, buy one....a full length one. There is some strange relationship between **changing into your jeans** and **not making supper**. If you really want work to end, end your work before you change!!

Timer

The best investment I ever made for lowering stress at supper time is an electronic timer. **It's for timing you**, not the food. **When you time yourself** during the work week there is a **real beginning** and more importantly a **real end**. I say to my family, *"I've taken my stuff out and I'm setting the timer."* My family knows that means DO NOT DISTURB.

Terrific Helpers

There are some pretty terrific helpers out there, just waiting for you to appreciate them. I approached the companies you see listed on this page. **There is no financial compensation for using their names**, in fact it's quite a bit of red tape to have permission to use their names. Do you know why? **They needed to check me out** to make sure I didn't make them look bad - go figure! I really believe in them. There are many other great products out there, but these are some of my personal favorites. The following product and company names appearing in this book, in the recipes and in the grocery lists, are trademarks or trade names of their respective companies.

*Reg'd T.M. of Alberto-Culver Co.

Reg'd T.M. of ConAgra Grocery Products Limited

Reg'd T.M. of
McCain Foods Limited

CATELLI®, CATELLI BISTRO®, GARDEN SELECT®, and CATELLI with accompanying rainbow design® are registered trademarks of BF Foods International Corporation.

Alcan is a registered trademark of Alcan Inc.

Reg'd T.M. of The Holmes Group, Inc.

Reg'd T.M. of Fiesta Barbeques Limited

Our Guidelines for Selecting Ingredients

Vegetables and fruits are medium size unless otherwise specified.
Herbs and spices are dry. You can purchase dried herbs two ways - ground or leaves.
We use leaves unless otherwise specified.

Adjusting Nutritional Data

- All of the recipes in <u>Getting Ya Through The Summer</u> provide 4-6 servings.
- We chose the suggested serving sizes.
- Our test families varied in size. Some families said there was way too much food for 4 people, some thought it was just right.
- If you have 4 adults in your home with very healthy appetites the recipe will probably serve 4, (sometimes someone gets a left-over lunch the next day).
- If you have younger children the recipe will probably serve 6.
- When a range is given for the number of servings a recipe makes, the higher number is used (eg. 4-6 servings - data is supplied for 6 servings, including food choices).

Adjusting data when a recipe serves 4 instead of 6

# of g fat x 1.5 = # of g fat
eg. 12 g fat x 1.5 = 18 g fat
(12 g fat per serving for 6 servings) = (18 g fat per serving for 4 servings)

The formula works for calories, proteins, carbohydrates and fats.

Write this new information right on the recipe. Cross out the old and put in the new.
Mark the book, just like you would a daytimer. That's why we chose this type of binding.
This is the way to monitor your fat intake for the day. You need the proper information.

Feel great about staying on top of your health.

Weights and Measures

- Imperial and Metric conversions are approximate only.
- When weights or measures are provided in both Imperial and Metric, nutritional data is calculated using the Metric measure.
- When liquid measures are provided in Imperial, the Canadian measure is used.
- When a choice of two ingredients are listed (eg. pork or chicken), the first ingredient is used for the data.
- Ingredients listed as optional are not included in nutritional data.
- Rice has no butter added even when instructions on package suggest to do so.
- When using cooking spray we assume a 3 second spray using canola oil.

Produce

Broccoli floret - small	.2 oz	/ 50 g
Carrot (large)	.3-1/2 oz	/ 100 g
Cucumber (English)	.16 oz	/ 450 g
Lettuce (head) or spinach (bunch) 7-1/2 cups edible leaves	.7-1/2 oz	/ 216 g
large (10 cups edible leaves)	.10 oz	/ 288 g
small (3-3/4 cups edible leaves)	.4 oz	/ 108 g
Kiwi - small	.1-1/2 oz	/ 45 g
Onion	.6 oz	/ 180 g
small	.4 oz	/ 120 g
large	.8 oz	/ 240 g
Pepper - red or green	.7 oz	/ 200 g
Potato - large	.8 oz	/ 250 g
Tomato	.4 oz	/ 120 g
Zucchini	.7 oz	/ 210 g
small	.4 oz	/ 125 g

Baking Goods

Baguette	.12 oz	/ 350 g
Bun (multigrain)	.1-1/2 oz	/ 45 g
Bun (whole wheat)	.2 oz	/ 60 g
Dinner roll	.1 oz	/ 30 g
French loaf	.16 oz	/ 450 g
Pizza base - deli	.12 oz	/ 350 g

Dairy

Cheese (grated) 1 cup	.3-1/2 oz	/ 100 g
Cheddar cheese (low-fat)		6 % mf
Parmesan cheese		17 % mf

Meat

Chicken - precooked roaster (2.2 lbs or 1 kg) actual meat	.21 oz	/ 600 g
Pork ribs (raw weight 3 lbs or 1350 g) cook weight	.2 lbs	/ 900 g

Equipment List:	Per serving:	
BBQ	Calories	436
BBQ tools	Fat	6.4 g
Small microwave-safe pot	Protein	32.4 g
w/lid	Carbohydrate	62.2 g
Mixing bowl		
Cutting board		
Colander		
Sharp veggie knife		
Lge mixing spoon		
Measuring cups & spoons		

Prep Time

Food Choices:

2	Starch
1 1/2	Fruits + Veg
0	Milk 1%
1/2	Sugars
3	Protein
1	Fat
0	Extras

Equipment List

When we say, "Don't change yet! Take out equipment." on the recipe, we're referring to don't change your work clothes. It's amazing how following this advice will reduce your stress.

Food Analysis

If you flip through the book, you will notice all the food data is displayed clearly on the top right hand corner near the clock which indicates speed. This is designed so that you can immediately see your fat intake for the meal you've chosen for supper. It tells you at the beginning of the day what you should be eating during the day.

Eg: If supper has 6 grams of fat and you know your daily fat intake should be 67 grams (based on a 2000 calorie intake), then you know you have 61 grams to play with during the day. That's a lot. If you know, on the other hand, your supper is 25 grams of fat (our highest) you have to watch your fat intake a little more closely during the day. This keeps you balanced, always!

Diabetic Food Choices and Why!

Because a very large number of people have some form of diabetes, we feel it is important to include this information as well as the detailed nutritional analysis. Our recipes have very high standards for taste, speed and nutrition. It seems only fair to allow a person with diabetes the luxury of being able to use a regular cookbook with great tasting meals. They can simply adjust components according to their specific dietary requirements. There is another very important reason for having food choices. Some people use food choices rather than traditional food analysis to monitor weight gain.

Health Canada Sante Canada

CANADA'S
Food Guide

TO HEALTHY EATING
FOR PEOPLE FOUR YEARS AND OVER

Enjoy a variety
of foods from each
group every day.

Choose lower-
fat foods
more often.

Grain Products
Choose whole grain
and enriched
products more often.

Vegetables and Fruit
Chose dark green and
orange vegetables and
orange fruit more often.

Milk Products
Choose lower-fat milk
products more often.

Meat and Alternatives
Chose leaner meats,
poultry and fish as well
as dried peas, beans
and lentils more often.

Canada

- ✔ This is a workbook. Write in it! It will look like mine after a while with little splat marks all over it!

- ✔ The rating space is not for decoration. Write in your family rating for future reference.

- ✔ Change the grams of fat data according to how many servings your family eats (see page 27). This is an easy way to monitor your fat intake, daily.

- ✔ You may want to use this book just for the great recipes! If so, you're in for a big treat! But ... I challenge you - try one grocery list for one week, any week - and watch your stress level drop!

Recipes

SUPPERTIME!

Things You Should Know About the Recipes

Green

Oh, Oh, Oh, Oh!!!! Ron actually created this recipe! Boy does that guy know his flavors! (I taught him everything he knows!) Remember, our test families tell us that if you have a smaller BBQ with a flame close to the pan, you will need to use the heavy-duty foil for your diffuser <u>and</u> reduce the heat a little. Always preheat your BBQ to avoid burning.

Yellow

These are one of the best chicken burgers you may ever have! (Do you think I like this book?) To make this a vegetarian meal, grilled zucchini in this sauce is amazing. Add a little cheese for protein!

Blue

This is a fantastic "I cook, you clean" meal. The flavor of this beef is just amazing! It is a joy to come home and have this fantastic smell in your home, with no heat! If it's a super-hot day, you can roll up this beef in a pita and serve it with a cold salad. If you do this, remember to make the adjustments on your photocopied grocery list.

Red Wings

If you are a vegetarian, try this salad with cheese chunks for protein or use some toasted almonds, pine nuts or seeds.

Yellow Wings

This has a fantastic flavor. If you like it veggie version, firm tofu is fabulous with this!

Week 1

Green: Plum Chicken with Singapore
Noodles and Asparagus

Our Family Rating: 9.5
Your Family Rating: _____

Yellow: Honey-Mustard Chicken Burgers
with Fresh Fruit Salad

Our Family Rating: 10
Your Family Rating: _____

Blue: BBQ Style Beef with Corn Salad
and Grilled Potatoes

Our Family Rating: 8
Your Family Rating: _____

Red Wings: Cajun Chicken Caesar Salad

Our Family Rating: 10
Your Family Rating: _____

Yellow Wings: Beef and Broccoli with Rice

Our Family Rating: 10
Your Family Rating: _____

Plum Chicken with Singapore Noodles and Asparagus

Instructions:

Don't change yet. Take out equipment.
1. Fill your **kettle** full of water and boil.
   <u>Preheat BBQ</u> to med (approx 350° F).

2. Spray a large cake pan with cooking spray. Unravel chicken thighs and lay flat on pan. Combine the following in a small bowl in this order; cornstarch, gradually mix in hoisin so cornstarch is smooth not lumpy. Blend in plum sauce, soy, peach jam, water, ginger, lemon juice and hot chili sauce. Pour evenly over the chicken.

   Place <u>uncovered</u> pan on foil diffuser (see page 3) in **preheated BBQ**. <u>Close lid.</u> Set timer for 30 min.

3. Rinse noodles in a colander. Place in a large heatproof bowl or pot. Cover with boiling water and <u>let stand</u> while preparing asparagus.

4. Wash asparagus and place in a heap on a large piece of sprayed foil (shiny side in). Salt lightly. Do the "Wrap" (see page 3) and set aside until timer rings for BBQ.

5. Drain noodles in a colander.
   In the <u>uncleaned</u> mixing bowl combine chicken broth, honey, curry and basil. Return noodles to bowl, toss and <u>set aside</u>.
   ...when timer rings...
6. Leave chicken in BBQ. Place asparagus on **BBQ grill**. Set timer for 15 minutes. Turn once.

7. Just before serving **microwave** noodles at high for 3 minutes or until hot.

50 Eating Time

Ingredients:

Take out equipment.
water

cooking spray (PAM)
10-12 boneless skinless chicken thighs (1-3/4 lbs or 800 g)
2 Tbsp cornstarch
1/4 cup <u>each</u> of <u>hoisin sauce,</u> <u>V-H plum sauce, soy sauce (V-H),</u> <u>peach jam</u> and <u>water</u>
1 tsp <u>each</u> of <u>ginger powder,</u> <u>lemon juice</u> and <u>hot chili sauce</u>

aluminum foil (Alcan)

1 lb or 450 g precooked vermicelli noodles usually found in the produce dept

aluminum foil (Alcan)
cooking spray (PAM)
16 stalks fresh asparagus (3/4 lb or 340 g)
1/2 tsp salt (optional)

1/4 cup chicken broth
1 Tbsp liquid honey
2 tsp curry powder
1/2 tsp basil leaves

Note Use deboned thighs only (as a shorter cooking time is best to keep these saucy).

When timer rings for noodles all is ready.

<u>**Serves 4-6**</u>

Equipment List:

BBQ
Kettle
Large cake pan
Small mixing bowl
Lge heatproof bowl or pot
Colander
Can opener
Lge mixing spoon
Pasta fork
Sharp veggie knife
Measuring cups & spoons

Per serving:

Calories	383
Fat	6.8 g
Protein	33.7 g
Carbohydrate	46.8 g

Food Choices:

1 1/2	Starch
0	Fruits + Veg
0	Milk 1%
2 1/2	Sugars
4 1/2	Protein
0	Fat
0	Extras

Prep Time

Plum Chicken

YELLOW

Honey-Mustard Chicken Burgers
with Fresh Fruit Salad

Instructions:

Don't change yet! Take out equipment.
1. <u>Preheat BBQ</u> to med (approx 350° F).

2. Wash fruit under cold water.

   Cut fruit into bite size pieces and place in serving bowl.

   Refrigerate until ready to eat.

   Place yogurt in small serving bowl and **refrigerate**.

3. Mix the following together in a large bowl; Dijon mustard, honey and spices

   Cut chicken breasts in half to make 8 pieces. Toss all 8 pieces into mustard bowl and keep lifting and mixing with a fork until all the pieces look glossy.

   Grill on the **BBQ**, <u>lid closed</u>, approx 5 minutes each side or <u>only until center is no longer pink</u>.
             ...meanwhile...
4. Prepare your favorite toppings.

5. Serve on buns with anything you choose.

   Option
   Sometimes I like to serve the fruit salad as an appetizer before cooking the chicken.

Ingredients:

Take out ingredients.

1/2 cantaloupe (3/4 lb or 350 g)
or any melon in season
1 bunch red or green grapes (3/4 lb or 350 g)
8 strawberries
2 small kiwi fruit

1 cup low-fat French vanilla yogurt

1/4 cup Dijon mustard
1/4 cup liquid honey
1/2 tsp <u>each</u> of <u>Mrs. Dash Italian Seasoning</u> and <u>Mrs. Dash Extra Spicy Seasoning</u>

4 large boneless skinless chicken breasts (1-1/2 lbs or 700 g)

mayonnaise, tomatoes, lettuce, slivered onions (optional)

4-6 multigrain buns

<u>Serves 4-6</u>

  Eating Time

36

Equipment List:

BBQ
BBQ tools
Lge mixing bowl
Small mixing bowl
Salad bowl
Cutting board
2 small mixing spoons
Sharp meat knife
Sharp veggie knife
Fork
Measuring cups & spoons

Per serving:

Calories	368
Fat	4.2 g
Protein	33.0 g
Carbohydrate	49.5 g

Food Choices:

1	Starch
1 1/2	Fruits + Veg
1/2	Milk 1%
1 1/2	Sugars
4	Protein
1/2	Fat
0	Extras

Prep Time

Honey-Mustard Chicken Burgers

BBQ Style Beef with Corn Salad and Grilled Potatoes

Instructions:

...the night before...
Take out equipment.
1. Cut meat into large chunks adding to **crockpot** as you cut. Sprinkle with flour and spice and stir to coat.

Chop onion and green pepper and add to crockpot.
Add ketchup, BBQ sauce, garlic and water. Place crock in **fridge** overnight.

...in the morning...
Return center pot <u>with cover</u> to the outer crock and set on **low heat**.
Go to work and have a lovely day.

...when you get home for supper...
2. **Preheat BBQ** to med (approx 350° F). Wash potatoes and cut in half lengthwise. Spray flat side of potato with cooking spray and sprinkle with spice. Wrap in foil shiny side in and place in **preheated BBQ** flat side down.
<u>Close lid</u>. Set timer for 25 minutes.

3. Chop tomatoes and green pepper.

In a salad bowl combine tomatoes, green pepper, corn, vinegar, oil, mustard and spices.

Stir until well mixed. <u>Cover</u> and **refrigerate** until serving.

...when timer rings...
Dinner is ready!

Ingredients:

...the night before...
Take out ingredients.
2 lbs or 900 g lean sirloin steak
2 Tbsp flour and
1-1/2 Tbsp <u>Mrs. Dash</u>
<u>Peppercorn Blend</u>

1 onion
1 green pepper
1/4 cup <u>each</u> of <u>ketchup</u> and <u>BBQ sauce</u> (use bottled or see back cover)
1 tsp prepared garlic
1 cup water
If you like things spicy add 1-2 tsp hot chili sauce.

4-6 large potatoes
cooking spray (PAM)
1 tsp paprika (for all)
1 tsp garlic powder (for all)
aluminum foil (Alcan)

2 med size tomatoes
1/2 green pepper
1 can corn drained (**14 oz or 398 mL**)
2 Tbsp red wine vinegar
1 Tbsp extra virgin olive oil
1/2 tsp <u>each</u> of <u>paprika</u> and <u>Dijon mustard</u>
1/8 tsp <u>each</u> of <u>cumin</u>, <u>black pepper</u> & <u>salt</u>

<u>Serves 4-6</u>

40 Eating Time

Equipment List:

...the night before...
Crock-pot
Cutting board
Sharp meat knife
Sharp vegetable knife
Lge mixing spoon
Measuring cups & spoons

...when you arrive home...
BBQ
Salad bowl
Cutting board
Lge mixing spoon
Sharp vegetable knife
Measuring spoons

Per serving:

Calories	428
Fat	8.3 g
Protein	39.1 g
Carbohydrate	49.2 g

Food Choices:

2 1/2	Starch
1/2	Fruits + Veg
0	Milk 1%
1/2	Sugars
5	Protein
1/2	Fat
0	Extras

Prep Time

BBQ Style Beef

Cajun Chicken Caesar Salad

Instructions:

Don't change yet. Take out equipment.
1. Tear lettuce into bite size pieces, place in salad spinner, rinse under cold water and spin dry.
   Transfer to salad bowl.
   Pour dressing as desired over salad and toss to coat.

   Sprinkle with bacon bits and croutons.
   Divide onto individual serving plates.

2. Peel cooked chicken off the roaster and cut into bite size pieces. Place in a microwave safe bowl.

   Toss with spice and cook in **microwave** at high about 2 minutes or until hot. Toss and heat again for 1 minute.

   Divide equally over lettuce and finish with a sprinkle of Parmesan!

3. Serve with multigrain buns.

   Deeeeeelicious!!!!

Ingredients:

Take out ingredients.
1 large head of Romaine lettuce

1/4 cup gourmet Caesar salad dressing mixed with 1/4 cup lowest-fat mayonnaise

2 Tbsp real bacon bits (optional)
1 cup croutons

1/2 of a (2.2 lbs or 1 kg) precooked roaster chicken
Option *You can buy 2/3 lb or 300 g boneless, skinless deli cooked chicken.*

2 tsp Mrs. Dash Extra Spicy Seasoning

1 Tbsp low-fat grated Parmesan cheese

4-6 multigrain buns

Serves 4-6

25 Eating Time

Equipment List:

Salad spinner
Lge mixing bowl
Med size microwave-safe
  bowl
2 large stirring spoons
Sharp meat knife
Measuring cups & spoons

Per serving:

Calories	267
Fat	11.0 g
Protein	19.6 g
Carbohydrate	22.5 g

Food Choices:

1	Starch
0	Fruits + Veg
0	Milk 1%
1/2	Sugars
2 1/2	Protein
1 1/2	Fat
0	Extras

Prep Time

Cajun Chicken

Beef and Broccoli with Rice

Instructions:

Don't change yet! Take out equipment.
1. Combine rice and water in a microwave-safe pot or casserole with lid. <u>Cover</u> and **microwave** at high 10 minutes, then medium 10 minutes.

2. Heat oil in a large nonstick fry pan or wok at med-high. Cut meat into thin strips against the grain and add to pan as you cut. Toss occasionally.
Add garlic, pepper and dried chili flakes.

Slice onion into thin strips and add to pan as you slice.
Wash and cut mushrooms in half adding to pan as you cut.
Wash and cut broccoli into bite size pieces adding to pan as you cut.
Wash and slice zucchini into long 1/2" thick sticks. Add to pan as you cut.

Combine the following in a small mixing bowl; brown sugar, soy, ginger-sesame-Thai sauce and V-H dry-garlic sauce.

Pour over meat and veggies until heated through and well coated.

...when timer rings for rice...
3. Let rice stand for about 5 minutes to set. ...then enjoy!!!

Ingredients:

Take out ingredients.
1-1/2 cups white or brown rice
3 cups water

1 tsp canola oil
1-1/2 lbs or 675 g lean sirloin steak

3 tsp prepared garlic
1 tsp <u>each</u> of <u>fresh ground pepper</u> and <u>dried chili flakes</u>

1 onion

10-12 fresh mushrooms

3 florets fresh broccoli

1 small zucchini

1 Tbsp <u>each</u> of <u>brown sugar</u> and <u>soy sauce</u> (V-H)
3 Tbsp ginger-sesame-Thai sauce
2 Tbsp V-H dry-garlic sauce

<u>Serves 4-6</u>

  Eating Time

Equipment List:

Lge nonstick fry pan or wok
Lge microwave-safe pot
  w/lid
Small mixing bowl
Cutting board
2 stirring spoons
Sharp meat knife
Sharp veggie knife
Measuring cups & spoons

Per serving:

Calories	372
Fat	6.2 g
Protein	29.6 g
Carbohydrate	49.6 g

Food Choices:

2 1/2	Starch
1/2	Fruits + Veg
0	Milk 1%
1	Sugars
3 1/2	Protein
1/2	Fat
0	Extras

Prep Time

Beef and Broccoli

Things You Should Know About the Recipes

Green

Don't flip out if the kids still want to plaster their steak with ketchup. You will get addicted to this sesame sauce if you are anything like us!

Red Wings

This is a unique way of making your own pizza in the hot summer. It's fun, you can make it the way you want, it's cheaper, and you can control things like the fat in the cheese, etc... For a veggie pizza, leave out the sauce for a change. Brush with olive oil and sprinkle with garlic powder. Add artichokes, onion, sun dried tomatoes and mushrooms. Sprinkle with feta and low fat mozza!

Yellow Wings

We played and played and played with this recipe until we got it! Most Beef Bourguignon has a very strong alcohol flavor...this one is just perfect. It may be an easy "I cook, you clean" meal but it qualifies for entertaining!

Blue

You will serve this to guests and they will think you've gone gourmet on them! Remember, our test families reminded us that if you have an older BBQ and the flame is close to the grill, make sure you use the heavy-duty foil for your diffuser and turn the heat down a little. Always preheat your BBQ to avoid burning!

Yellow

This is amazing and fast for those cloudy days. To have this meatless, just omit the pork or chicken and add firm tofu or you can add extra veggies and toss in cashews.

Green: Steak with Sesame Sauce, Baked Potatoes and Grilled Veggies

Our Family Rating: 8
Your Family Rating: _____

Red Wings: BBQ Pizza

Our Family Rating: 10
Your Family Rating: _____

Yellow Wings: Beef Bourguignon with Strawberry Spinach Salad

Our Family Rating: 8
Your Family Rating: _____

Blue: Quicky Chicken Florentine with Whole Wheat Couscous and Broccoli

Our Family Rating: 9.5
Your Family Rating: _____

Yellow: Sweet and Sour Pork (or Chicken) with Rice and Pineapple

Our Family Rating: 8.5
Your Family Rating: _____

2

Steak with Sesame Sauce, Baked Potatoes and Grilled Veggies

Instructions:

Don't change yet! Take out equipment.
1. <u>Preheat BBQ</u> to med (approx 350° F).

2. Wash potatoes and slice into 3 sections lengthwise. Wrap each potato in a sprayed piece of foil, shiny side in, after adding pepper and seasoning. Place in **preheated BBQ**. Set timer for 25 min.

3. Slice peppers, zucchini, onions and mushrooms in large chunks and as you chop place on a large piece of foil shiny side up.

   Dab with pesto and do a foil wrap (see page 3). <u>Set aside</u>.

4. Combine tahini, soy sauce, ginger, salt, paprika and garlic in a small bowl. **Microwave** at high for 10 seconds. Stir to blend while gradually adding mayo and water. Set aside on the dinner table. *It's to serve as a sauce beside the steak.*

   ...when timer rings for potatoes...
5. Leave potatoes in. Toss the foil wrap of veggies into the **BBQ**.
   Set timer for 15 minutes turning once.

   ...when timer rings again...
6. <u>Remove potatoes and veggies</u>...or store on top rack if you have one.

7. **Grill** steak on **BBQ** to desired wellness.

8. Add your favorite toppings to your baked potato.

Ingredients:

Take out ingredients.

4-6 large potatoes
aluminum foil (Alcan)
cooking spray (PAM)
fresh ground pepper
butter and seasoning (optional)

aluminum foil (Alcan)
1 red pepper
1 green pepper
1 small zucchini
1 onion
10 mushrooms
3 Tbsp prepared basil pesto

<u>Sesame Sauce</u>
1/4 cup tahini (ground sesame seeds, looks like peanut butter)
2 Tbsp soy sauce (V-H)
1/4 tsp <u>each</u> of <u>ground ginger</u> and <u>salt</u>
1/8 tsp paprika
1 tsp prepared garlic
1 Tbsp lowest-fat mayo
3 Tbsp water

1-1/2 lbs or 675 g lean sirloin beef

no-fat sour cream, butter, green onion, bacon bits (optional)

<u>Serves 4-6</u>

50 Eating Time

Equipment List:

BBQ
BBQ tongs
Small mixing bowl
Sharp veggie knife
Mixing spoon
Measuring cups
Measuring spoons

Per serving:

Calories	412
Fat	13.8 g
Protein	33.3 g
Carbohydrate	38.8 g

Food Choices:

2	Starch
1	Fruits + Veg
0	Milk 1%
0	Sugars
4	Protein
1 1/2	Fat
0	Extras

Prep Time

Steak with Sesame Sauce

BBQ Pizza

Instructions:

Don't change yet! Take out equipment.
1. <u>Preheat BBQ</u> to med-low (approx 300° F).

Spread sauce over crusts as desired with a spoon or spatula and sprinkle with spice.

If you like a more interesting pizza... check out some alternate suggestions on the recipe description page and adjust your photocopied grocery list.

Chop ham, pepper, onion and mushrooms into small pieces and distribute evenly over crusts.

Sprinkle with cheese.

Place pizzas on foil diffuser (see page 3) on **preheated BBQ**.
<u>Close lid</u>. They only take a few minutes.

Check often ...
When bottom crusts are browned... pizzas are ready.

Ingredients:

Take out ingredients.

2 12" bakery pizza crusts
Depending on the surface size of your BBQ you may have to cut them in 1/2 before you begin to ensure they fit.
1 cup or 250 mL Catelli pizza sauce *Use Spicy Garlic & Onion if you like more zip.*
2 tsp Mrs. Dash Italian Seasoning

4-6 slices deli lean cooked ham (7 oz or 200 g)
1 small green pepper
1 small onion
6-8 mushrooms

2 cups grated part-skim mozzarella cheese

aluminum foil (Alcan)

If you like things spicy sprinkle with crushed chilies or Mrs. Dash Extra Spicy Seasoning.

<u>**Serves 4-6**</u>

  Eating Time

Equipment List:

BBQ
Cheese grater
Spatula or spoon
Sharp meat knife
Sharp veggie knife
Measuring spoons

Per serving:

Calories	487
Fat	10.7 g
Protein	29.4 g
Carbohydrate	68.4 g

Food Choices:

4	Starch
1/2	Fruits + Veg
0	Milk 1%
1/2	Sugars
3	Protein
1/2	Fat
0	Extras

Prep Time

2

BBQ Pizza

Beef Bourguignon with Strawberry Spinach Salad

Instructions:

...the night before...

Take out equipment.

1. Heat oil in a large nonstick fry pan at med-high.

Cut beef into 1" large cubes and toss into fry pan as you cut. <u>Brown</u> until outside of cubes are a nice dark brown.

Microwave brandy 10 seconds then pour into a metal ladle and light with a match. Pour the lit brandy over the beef and wait until the flame goes out. Toss beef into the **crockpot**.

Brown whole washed mushrooms and onions for a few minutes in the uncleaned pan adding the butter. Now toss into crock with the meat.

In the uncleaned pan (**no heat**) add the following in this order; cornstarch, gradually blend in tomato paste, sherry, water, beef broth, bay leaf, pepper and parsley. Stir until bottom of pan comes clean. Pour into crock with meat. Store centre crock in the **<u>fridge</u>** overnight.

...in the morning...

Return center pot <u>with cover</u> to the outer crock and set on **low heat**.

...when you get home for supper...

2. Prepare poppyseed dressing on back cover.

Rinse spinach in salad spinner under cold water and spin dry. Wash and slice strawberries then toss with spinach in a large bowl. Sprinkle with bacon bits. Toss with dressing as desired to coat.

3. Serve with your favorite bread.

Ingredients:

...the night before...

Take out ingredients.

1 tsp canola oil

2 lbs or 900 g lean sirloin or round steak

3 Tbsp brandy *This step is optional, however, the true beef bourguignon flavor comes out when adding the lit brandy.*

15 whole small mushrooms
15 pearl onions
...or 2 small onions cut in quarters
1 tsp butter

3 Tbsp cornstarch *Use more cornstarch for a thicker broth.*
2 Tbsp tomato paste *I freeze the rest.*
1 cup sherry *...or add 2 Tbsp brown sugar to 1 cup red wine*
1 cup water
1 can beef broth undiluted
(10 oz or 284 mL)
1 bay leaf
1 tsp pepper
1 tsp dried parsley

1/3 cup poppyseed dressing
(see back cover or use bottled)
1 pkg washed baby spinach
(10 oz or 284 g)
6 fresh strawberries
2 Tbsp real bacon bits (optional)

4-6 slices whole wheat bread
<u>Serves 4-6</u>

25 Eating Time

Equipment List:

...the night before...
Crockpot
Lge nonstick fry pan
Metal ladle
Lge mixing spoon
Sharp meat & veggie knives
Measuring cups & spoons
Matches

...when you get home...
Salad spinner
Salad bowl & spoons
Small bowl and spoon
Sharp veggie knife
Measuring spoons

Per serving:

Calories	371
Fat	13.2 g
Protein	38.0 g
Carbohydrate	25.0 g

Food Choices:

1/2	Starch
1/2	Fruits + Veg
0	Milk 1%
1	Sugars
5	Protein
2	Fat
0	Extras

Prep Time

2

Beef Bourguignon

Quicky Chicken Florentine with Whole Wheat Couscous and Broccoli

Instructions:

Don't change yet! Take out equipment.
1. <u>Preheat BBQ</u> to med (approx 350° F).
   Spray a 9"x9" cake pan with cooking spray. Squeeze the moisture from the spinach in a colander using a fork. Sprinkle with spice.
   Cut each breast in half. Make a slice down the center of each half, not cutting all the way through.
   Place each piece, **slit side up**, in the palm of your hand. Spoon a tiny bit of spinach on top. Flip the piece, **chicken side up**, onto the cake pan. Repeat with all the chicken.

   Mix in a bowl in this order; soup, mayo, garlic powder, celery salt and curry powder. Stir until smooth. Spoon over chicken.

   In a different bowl mix breadcrumbs, Parmesan, parsley and oil together. Sprinkle over the chicken and sauce. Place pan on foil diffuser (see pg. 3) in **preheated BBQ**. Set timer for 35 minutes. <u>Close lid.</u>

2. Rinse broccoli under cold water in a colander. Place in med size microwave-safe pot or casserole with lid. <u>Cover</u> and **microwave** on high for 5 minutes. When timer rings for chicken **turn BBQ to low and leave it in.**

3. Make couscous in a **stove-top** pot according to package directions. When the couscous is ready so is the chicken.

4. Stir broccoli and **microwave** at high for 2 additional minutes <u>just before serving</u>.

Ingredients:

Take out ingredients.

cooking spray (PAM)
4 oz or 115 g frozen chopped spinach
1/2 tsp Mrs. Dash Original Seasoning
4 large boneless skinless chicken breasts (1-1/2 lbs or 675 g)
If some of the spinach falls out or these don't look perfect, don't worry, this meal looks fantastic after it's baked.

1 can (10 oz or 284 mL) cream of mushroom soup
1/2 cup lowest-fat mayonnaise
1/4 tsp garlic powder
1/8 tsp celery salt
1/2 Tbsp curry powder

1/2 cup fine breadcrumbs
3-1/2 Tbsp grated low-fat Parmesan cheese
1 tsp dried parsley
1/2 Tbsp canola oil
aluminum foil (Alcan)

4 cups frozen cut broccoli

1-1/2 cups whole-wheat couscous
We like to add 1 Tbsp salsa, 1 tsp cilantro and chicken broth for part of the liquid.

Serves 4-6

  Eating Time

Equipment List:

BBQ
Med-size microwave-safe
  pot w/lid
Med-size stove-top pot
  w/lid
Colander
9"x9" cake pan
2 small mixing bowls
Can opener
Sharp meat knife
2 mixing spoons
Fork & spoon
Measuring cups & spoons

Per serving:

Calories	460
Fat	10.8 g
Protein	41.0 g
Carbohydrate	49.6 g

Food Choices:

2 1/2	Starch
0	Fruits + Veg
0	Milk 1%
1	Sugars
5	Protein
1 1/2	Fat
0	Extras

Prep Time

2

Quicky Chicken Florentine

Sweet and Sour Pork (or Chicken) with Rice and Pineapple

Instructions:

Don't change yet! Take out equipment.
1. Combine rice and water in a microwave-safe pot or casserole dish with lid.
   <u>Cover</u> and **microwave** at high 10 minutes, then medium 10 minutes.

2. Heat oil in a large nonstick fry pan or wok at med-high. Add garlic.

   Cut pork or chicken into thin strips and gradually add to pan as you cut.

   …meanwhile…
   Slice onion and green pepper into strips. Add to pan as you slice. Toss occasionally.

   Combine cornstarch with soy in a small bowl. *Gradually add soy while stirring with a fork so the cornstarch is smooth not lumpy.*
   Mix in juice from pineapple, sugar and vinegar.
   Add to fry pan and stir until thickened.

   Option
   You can slice some of the pineapple directly into the sauce and serve some on each plate for a fresh summer look.

Ingredients:

Take out ingredients.
3 cups water
1-1/2 cups white rice

1 tsp canola oil
2 tsp prepared garlic

1 lb or 450 g boneless trimmed pork chops *This is also excellent with boneless skinless chicken.*

1 small onion
1 small green pepper
If you like things spicy add hot chili flakes to this step.

2 Tbsp cornstarch
4 Tbsp soy sauce (V-H)

juice from a (14 oz or 398 mL) can of unsweetened pineapple
2 Tbsp <u>each</u> of <u>brown sugar</u> and <u>vinegar</u>

pineapple slices

<u>Serves 4-6</u>

  Eating Time

Equipment List:

Lge nonstick fry pan or wok
Lge microwave-safe pot
  w/lid
Small mixing bowl
Can opener
Lge mixing spoon
Sharp meat knife
Sharp veggie knife
Fork
Measuring cups & spoons

Per serving:

Calories	369
Fat	5.9 g
Protein	21.2 g
Carbohydrate	57.0 g

Food Choices:

2 1/2	Starch
1 1/2	Fruits + Veg
0	Milk 1%
1/2	Sugars
2 1/2	Protein
0	Fat
0	Extras

Prep Time

Sweet and Sour Pork

Things You Should Know
About the Recipes

Yellow Wings Fabulous meal!!!! TIP If you don't have time to skewer the chicken, the Foil Buddies from Alcan work beautifully. Just lay the chicken strips on top and cook, turning once, until no longer pink.

Red This is a fantastic mealtime salad and got rave reviews from our test families. Our kids like it best when we use the plan ahead tip on the recipe. To make this a veggie dish replace the beef with nuts and seeds.

Green All of our test families loved this meal. Not all of their kids liked the spaghetti squash. Serving this with either baked potatoes or rice is a way to keep the house cool and it's amazing with either.

Red Wings I'm not always fond of tortellini ...sometimes it's just too heavy a meal, buuut this soup is absolutely to die for!!! Whether you are a tortellini fan or not, this will become a favorite. This "I cook, you clean" meal takes about 5 minutes to prep once you have all your stuff out! Relace the chicken broth with vegetable broth to make a veggie meal.

Blue This is one of my favorite rib recipes. When you do this as an "I cook, you clean" meal...it makes it even more enjoyable. You come home to these marinated lick your lips ribs that are all ready to go!

Week 3

Yellow Wings: Thai Satay with Rice in
Lettuce Leaves

Our Family Rating: 10
Your Family Rating: _____

Red: Asian Beef Mealtime Salad

Our Family Rating: 8.5
Your Family Rating: _____

Green: Chicken Cacciatore with Garlic
Bread and Spaghetti Squash

Our Family Rating: 8.5
Your Family Rating: _____

Red Wings: Vegetable Tortellini Soup with
Whole Wheat Crackers

Our Family Rating: 10
Your Family Rating: _____

Blue: Texas Style BBQ Pork Ribs
with Grilled Vegetables

Our Family Rating: 9
Your Family Rating: _____

3

Thai Satay with Rice in Lettuce Leaves

Instructions:

Don't change yet! Take out equipment.
1. Combine soy sauce, brown sugar, garlic
   and cayenne pepper in a mixing bowl.
   Cut chicken into long strips (approx 5 strips
   per breast) and add to soy mixture as you
   slice. Submerge and let soak in **fridge**.
   Soak skewers in water.

   Preheat BBQ to medium (approx 350° F).

2. Combine rice and water in a large
   microwave-safe pot or casserole with lid.
   <u>Cover</u> and **microwave** at high 10 minutes,
   then medium 10 minutes.

3. Rinse <u>whole lettuce leaves</u> under cold
   water, pat dry with a paper towel and
   refrigerate until serving.
   Make a mixture of brown sugar, dressing
   and crushed chilies in a small bowl.
   <u>Set aside on serving table</u>.

4. Place peanut butter in a small microwave-
   safe bowl. Soften in **microwave** 20-25
   seconds or until it's slightly runny. Add
   soy, brown sugar, spices and water. Keep
   stirring with fork until well blended. Add
   water until smooth and just a little runny.
   <u>Set aside on serving table</u>.

   Skewer chicken and **grill** on **BBQ,** turning
   once, until meat is no longer pink.
   (This only takes a few minutes.)

   Tip
   See page 56 for a time-saving option.

Ingredients:

Take out ingredients.
1/2 cup soy sauce (V-H)
1/8 cup brown sugar
1 tsp prepared garlic (in a jar)
1/8 tsp cayenne pepper
**4 large boneless skinless chicken
breasts (1-1/2 lbs or 675 g)**
bamboo skewers

1-1/2 cups basmati rice
3 cups water

**1 bunch green leaf or Romaine
lettuce**

1/4 cup brown sugar
**3/4 cup sundried tomato and
oregano salad dressing**
1/8 tsp chili flakes

**1-1/2 Tbsp lower-fat creamy
peanut butter**
1 Tbsp soy sauce (V-H)
1 tsp brown sugar
**1/8 tsp <u>each</u> of <u>cumin powder</u>
and <u>cayenne pepper</u>**
water to smooth (approx 2 tsp)

bamboo skewers

*The peanut sauce is to spread
sparingly on the chicken. The
dressing is to drizzle on the rice.
Roll the rice up in the leaf like a
taco... or you can just cut it all up
and eat it with a knife and fork...
either way it's amazing!!!*

(25) Eating Time   **Serves 4-6**

Equipment List:

BBQ
Lge microwave-safe pot
  w/lid
Medium size mixing bowl
2 small mixing bowls
Fork
Skewers (bamboo)
Measuring cups & spoons

Per serving:

Calories	449
Fat	12.3 g
Protein	33.9 g
Carbohydrate	50.7 g

Food Choices:

2	Starch
0	Fruits + Veg
0	Milk 1%
2	Sugars
4 1/2	Protein
2	Fat
0	Extras

Prep Time

3

Thai Satay

Asian Beef Mealtime Salad

Instructions:

Don't change yet! Take out equipment.
1. Rinse spinach leaves under cold water in salad spinner and spin dry. Divide evenly on individual serving plates.

   Prepare honey-mustard dressing on back cover or use bottled.

   Set aside in **fridge**.

   Slice celery and green onion (finely) and scatter on top of spinach.

   Cut cucumber and carrot into matchstick strips and scatter on top as well.

   <u>Drizzle with dressing</u> as desired.

2. Place sliced beef evenly on top of salad.

3. Serve with multigrain buns.

Option
I like to rinse bean sprouts and scatter them on top as a garnish... and we even like the flavor it adds to the salad.

Plan Ahead Tip
*Smother a thick lean boneless steak with Mrs. Dash Peppercorn Blend.
Cook on the grill while the BBQ is being used for another meal. Thin slice then freeze or refrigerate (depending on when you are serving it). ...or set aside some of the awesome BBQ roast from page 72.*

Ingredients:

Take out ingredients.
**1 bag baby spinach leaves
(10 oz or 284 g)**

1/2 cup honey-mustard dressing
(see back cover or use bottled)

**1 stalk celery
2 green onions**

**1/2 English cucumber
1 large carrot**

**12 slices med-rare deli roast beef
thinly sliced (1/2 lb or 225 g)**

4-6 multigrain buns

1 cup fresh bean sprouts
(optional)

<u>Serves 4-6</u>

 Eating Time

Equipment List:

Salad spinner
Small mixing bowl
Cutting board
Mixing spoon
Sharp veggie knife
Measuring cups & spoons

Per serving:

Calories	215
Fat	5.5 g
Protein	16.5 g
Carbohydrate	24.8 g

Food Choices:

1	Starch
1/2	Fruits + Veg
0	Milk 1%
1/2	Sugars
2	Protein
1/2	Fat
0	Extras

Prep Time

3

Asian Beef Mealtime Salad

Chicken Cacciatore with Garlic Bread and Spaghetti Squash

Instructions:

Don't change yet! Take out the equipment.
1. <u>Preheat BBQ</u> to med (approx 350° F).

2. Cut squash in half lengthwise, remove seeds and place each half on it's own large piece of sprayed foil, shiny side up.

   Sprinkle each half with brown sugar, salt and curry. Close foil tightly and set aside.

3. Unravel chicken thighs and lay flat in a large oven-safe sprayed cake pan.

   Sprinkle with brown sugar, finely chopped celery, and mushrooms.

   Blend together in a small bowl; soup, salsa, onion flakes and spice.

   Spoon sauce over each thigh and sprinkle with mozzarella.

   Place cake pan on foil diffuser (see page 3) in **preheated BBQ**. Place squash in **BBQ**. <u>Close the lid.</u>
   Set timer for 35 minutes.

4. Slice bread lengthwise. Butter and sprinkle with garlic powder and dried parsley. When timer rings check squash with a fork. If tender rewrap and set aside, otherwise return to grill until chicken is ready. Reset timer 10 minutes until chicken is done. When chicken is ready **turn one side of BBQ off** and place the bread in the **BBQ** butter side up for just a few minutes on the side with no flame.

Ingredients:

Take out the ingredients.

1 spaghetti squash*
(2.2 lbs or 1 kg)
aluminum foil (Alcan)
cooking spray (PAM)
2 Tbsp brown sugar
1/2 tsp <u>each</u> of <u>salt</u> and <u>curry powder</u>

cooking spray (PAM)
10-12 boneless skinless chicken thighs (1-3/4 lb or 800 g)
3 Tbsp brown sugar (for all)
1 stalk celery
1 can sliced mushrooms (drained) **(10 oz or 284 mL)**

1 can tomato soup (10 oz or 284 mL)
1/2 of the soup can salsa
1 Tbsp onion flakes
1-1/2 tsp Mrs. Dash Italian Seasoning (for all)
Add hot chili sauce if you like things spicy.
1/2 cup grated mozzarella cheese
aluminum foil (Alcan)

1 baguette or French loaf
3 Tbsp butter
2 tsp <u>each</u> of <u>garlic powder</u> and <u>dried parsley</u>

*Note
If it's difficult to find spaghetti squash this meal is fabulous with baked potatoes as well.

Use deboned thighs only (as a shorter cooking time is best to keep these saucy).

<u>Serves 4-6</u>

50 Eating Time

Equipment List:

BBQ
Lge oven-safe cake pan
Cutting board
Cheese grater
Lge bread knife
Sharp veggie knife
Butter knife
Measuring cups & spoons

Per serving:

Calories	519
Fat	13.3 g
Protein	37.5 g
Carbohydrate	62.4 g

Food Choices:

2	Starch
2 1/2	Fruits + Veg
0	Milk 1%
1	Sugars
4 1/2	Protein
1 1/2	Fat
0	Extras

Prep Time

3

Chicken Cacciatore

Vegetable Tortellini Soup with Whole Wheat Crackers

Instructions:

...the night before...

Take out equipment.

1. Chop onion and celery (finely) adding to **crockpot** as you cut.

   Add to pot in this order; chicken broth, pasta sauce, garlic, spice, vegetables and water.

   I add the water to the empty jar of sauce, give it a shake and then add it to the pot.

   Stir together and store overnight in the **fridge**.

...in the morning...

Return centre pot <u>with cover</u> to the outer crock and set at **low heat**.

...when you get home for supper...

Add tortellini to the pot and set timer for 15 minutes.

Now... go get into your shorts... 'cause supper is ready baby!!!!

Note

I like to serve this with whole-wheat crackers. This is a light supper, but very filling!

Ingredients:

...the night before...

Take out ingredients.

1 onion
1 lge stalk celery

1 large tetrapak chicken broth (30 oz or 900 mL)
1 jar Catelli Garden Select pasta sauce *Country Mushroom* **(24.5 oz or 700 mL)**
2 tsp <u>each</u> of <u>prepared garlic</u> and <u>Mrs. Dash Italian Seasoning</u>
2 cups frozen mixed veggies
1 cup water
If you like food with a little extra kick add 1 tsp chili flakes.

4-5 cups fresh cheese tortellini

whole-wheat crackers (optional)

It's a nice touch to sprinkle low-fat Parmesan on top of each bowl of soup just before serving.

<u>**Serves 4-6**</u>

  Eating Time

Equipment List:

...the night before...
Crockpot
Cutting board
Can opener
Lge mixing spoon
Sharp vegetable knife
Measuring cups & spoons

Per serving:

Calories	271
Fat	5.6 g
Protein	15.4 g
Carbohydrate	39.6 g

Food Choices:

1 1/2	Starch
1 1/2	Fruits + Veg
0	Milk 1%
0	Sugars
1 1/2	Protein
1/2	Fat
0	Extras

Prep Time

Vegetable Tortellini Soup

Texas Style BBQ Pork Ribs with Grilled Vegetables

Instructions:

...the night before...
Take out equipment.
1. Mix the following together in a large bowl or container; ketchup, brown sugar, onion flakes, cider vinegar, Worcestershire, chili powder, hot chili sauce, bay leaf, water and light beer.

Slice ribs into strips and submerge in sauce. Leave overnight in **fridge**.

...when you arrive home for supper...
2. **Preheat BBQ** to med (approx 350° F).

3. Place each corn on the cob on a sprayed piece of aluminum foil. Drizzle with 1 Tbsp water. Wrap and set aside.

4. Place marinated ribs on **BBQ grill**. **Sear** each side. **Reduce BBQ heat** to low-med (300° F). Set timer for 15 minutes. Turn often brushing remaining marinade on ribs.

5. Slice and heap in the middle of 1 or 2 large pieces of foil <u>shiny side up</u>: peppers, onion, asparagus and mushrooms. Drizzle with olive oil and sprinkle with spice. Seal tightly and <u>set both foil packs aside</u>.

...when timer rings...
...while ribs are still cooking...

6. Place wrapped corn and veggie sacks on top rack of grill.
Reset timer for 20 minutes. Turn once. When timer rings all is ready.

50 Eating Time

Ingredients:

...the night before...
Take out ingredients.
1-1/2 cups ketchup
3 Tbsp brown sugar
2 Tbsp each of onion flakes, cider vinegar and Worcestershire sauce
1 tsp chili powder
2 tsp hot chili sauce
1 bay leaf
1/2 cup each of water and light beer (can be non-alcoholic)
3 lbs or 1350 g lean pork or beef ribs

aluminum foil (Alcan)
cooking spray (PAM)
4-6 corn on the cob
(husks removed)

aluminum foil (Alcan)
1 red pepper
1 onion
10 mushrooms
16 stalks of asparagus
1 tsp extra virgin olive oil
1 tsp Mrs. Dash Garlic & Herb Seasoning

Note   If you don't have a top rack, turn one side of the grill off. Keep the ribs on the flame side and veggies on the nonflame side.

Serves 4-6

66

Equipment List:

...the night before...
Large bowl
Cutting board
Sharp meat knife
Sharp veggie knife
Fork
Measuring cups & spoons

...when you get home...
BBQ
BBQ tools
Sharp veggie knife
Measuring spoons

Per serving:

Calories	510
Fat	24.0 g
Protein	23.1 g
Carbohydrate	50.5 g

Food Choices:

1	Starch
1	Fruits + Veg
0	Milk 1%
2 1/2	Sugars
3	Protein
3 1/2	Fat
0	Extras

Prep Time

Texas Style BBQ Pork Ribs

Things You Should Know About the Recipes

Red Wings

This amazing salad is extremely filling and just the right amount for a very hot day!! To make this a veggie dish, you can grill firm tofu then toss in the spice as you would with the chicken or for an easier version add chunks of cheese.

Blue

What can I say. This is an amazing way to serve a roast!

Yellow Wings

You may never want to go back to a longer version of chicken noodle soup again. To make this a veggie dish, omit the chicken, add firm tofu and use a vegetable broth instead.

Red

This can be done as a foil for those extremely unpredictable hot days. Follow the wrap instructions on page 3. Remember to use the heavy-duty variety of foil. Double wrap with the seam on the opposite side of the first so you don't lose the sauce. Put the bean sprouts in toward the end of cooking. This is beautiful with nuts, firm tofu or extra veggies instead of the meat.

Green

About a 5 minute prep in the kitchen folks!!! Remember our test families advise that if you have a smaller BBQ, you have to be using the heavy-duty foil for your diffuser and turn the heat down a little. Always preheat your BBQ, to avoid burning.

Week 4

Red Wings:　　　Fruity Chicken Mealtime Salad

> Our Family Rating: 9
> Your Family Rating: _____

Blue:　　　BBQ Roast with Baked Potatoes
　　　　　　　　and Mixed Veggies

> Our Family Rating: 8.5
> Your Family Rating: _____

Yellow Wings:　Chicken Noodle Soup with
　　　　　　　　Multigrain Buns

> Our Family Rating: 10
> Your Family Rating: _____

Red:　　　Beef Chow Mein Stir-Fry with Rice

> Our Family Rating: 8.5
> Your Family Rating: _____

Green:　　　Italian Baked Chicken with Garlic
　　　　　　　　Fusilli and Vegetables

> Our Family Rating: 9
> Your Family Rating: _____

4

Fruity Chicken Mealtime Salad

Instructions:

Don't change yet! Take out equipment.
1. Tear lettuce into bite size pieces and place in salad spinner. Rinse under cold water and spin dry.
   Arrange on individual serving plates.

   Mix together the following in a large bowl, in this order; mayonnaise, orange juice, sour cream, sugar, vinegar, curry powder, salt and pepper.

2. Peel cooked chicken from roaster and cut into bite-size pieces. Add to sauce in mixing bowl as you peel.

3. Peel avocado and cut into small pieces. Wash grapes and add both avocado and grapes to bowl. Toss until everything is coated and equally divide over lettuce leaves.

4. Serve with multigrain buns.

Tip
Finishing this off with orange or mandarin slices and sprinkling with a few walnuts or pine nuts is a really nice touch.

Ingredients:

Take out ingredients.
1 large bunch green leaf lettuce
(or butter lettuce as shown)

5 Tbsp lowest-fat mayonnaise
4 Tbsp orange juice (McCain)
3 Tbsp no-fat sour cream
1 Tbsp each of brown sugar and vinegar
1/2 tsp curry powder
1/4 tsp each of salt and pepper

1/2 of a (2.2 lb or 1 kg) precooked roaster chicken
Use the other 1/2 for the chicken noodle soup meal.
Option *You can buy 2/3 lb or 300 g boneless, skinless deli cooked chicken.*

1 large ripe avocado (2/3 lb or 300 g)
1/2 lb or 225 g red seedless grapes

4-6 multigrain buns

2 fresh mandarins or oranges (optional)
pine nuts, pecans or walnuts (optional)

Serves 4-6

(25) Eating Time

Equipment List:

Salad spinner
Lge mixing bowl
Lge mixing spoon
Sharp meat knife
Sharp veggie knife
Measuring spoons

Per serving:

Calories	288
Fat	9.7 g
Protein	17.5 g
Carbohydrate	32.6 g

Food Choices:

1	Starch
1	Fruits + Veg
0	Milk 1%
1/2	Sugars
2	Protein
1	Fat
0	Extras

Prep Time

Fruity Chicken Mealtime Salad

BBQ Roast with Baked Potatoes and Mixed Veggies

Instructions:

Don't change yet! Take out equipment.
1. <u>Preheat BBQ</u> to med (approx 350° F).

2. Sprinkle garlic all over roast.
   Sear all sides of roast in **BBQ**. <u>Close lid</u>.

   ...meanwhile...

3. Wash and wrap whole potatoes in foil shiny side in. Place in **BBQ**. <u>Close lid</u>.

4. Remove roast when seared on all sides and place on top of a large piece of foil, shiny side up.

   Finely chop onion.
   In a small bowl mix **only half** the chopped onion in with the BBQ sauce.
   Smother roast with BBQ sauce using a spatula or the back of a spoon. Close foil tightly around roast. **Turn flame off** on one side of BBQ. Place roast and potatoes on side with no flame. <u>Close lid</u>.

   If you can't turn flame off on one side, turn BBQ down to low-med (300° F).

   Set timer for 45 minutes.

5. Rinse vegetables in colander under cold water. Stir remaining chopped onion into veggie blend in a microwave-safe pot or casserole dish <u>with lid</u>. **Microwave** at high for 5 minutes, then let stand.

   When timer rings for roast and potatoes, **microwave** veggies 2 additional minutes, just before serving.

Ingredients:

Take out ingredients.

1 tsp garlic powder
1-1/2 lbs or 675 g beef sirloin roast

4-6 large potatoes
aluminum foil (Alcan)

aluminum foil (Alcan)

1 small onion (finely chopped)

1/2 cup BBQ sauce
(use bottled or see back cover)

4 cups frozen peas & carrots blend
remaining chopped onion

<u>Serves 4-6</u>

60 Eating Time

Equipment List:

BBQ
Microwave-safe pot w/lid
Cutting board
Colander
Spatula or spoon
Sharp veggie knife
Measuring cups

Per serving:

Calories	352
Fat	5.1 g
Protein	31.5 g
Carbohydrate	45.0 g

Food Choices:

2	Starch
1 1/2	Fruits + Veg
0	Milk 1%
0	Sugars
4	Protein
0	Fat
0	Extras

Prep Time

BBQ Roast

4

Chicken Noodle Soup with Multigrain Buns

Instructions:

...the night before...
Take out equipment.
1. Break roaster in half with a large knife. Remove meat from half the roaster, chop or break into pieces and place in **crockpot**.

Chop onion (finely), slice carrots and chop celery adding to pot as you cut.

Add to pot in this order; chicken broth, water, garlic, Worcestershire, soy, celery salt, poultry seasoning, pepper, hot chili sauce and Mrs. Dash.

Stir together and store overnight in the **fridge**.

...in the morning...
Return center pot <u>with cover</u> to the outer crock and set on **low heat**.
...aaaand bye bye... Have a nice day!
Cook between 5-10 hours.

...when you get home for supper...
2. Toss in the pasta and set your timer for 15 minutes!

3. Serve with multigrain buns.

Change into your shorts, have a cold shower... or whatever your little heart desires... beeeecause supper is ready, you organized little fiend you!!!!

Ingredients:

...the night before...
Take out ingredients.
<u>1/2 of a</u> **(2.2 lb or 1 kg) precooked roaster chicken from the grocery store**
(use the other 1/2 for the Fruity Chicken Salad meal)

1 onion
2 stalks celery
2 large carrots

2 large tetrapaks chicken broth (60 oz or 1.8L)
4 cups water
1 tsp <u>each</u> of <u>prepared garlic</u>, <u>Worcestershire sauce</u> and <u>soy sauce</u> (V-H)
1/4 tsp <u>each</u> of <u>celery salt</u>, <u>poultry seasoning</u>, <u>fresh ground pepper</u> and <u>hot chili sauce</u>
1/2 tsp Mrs. Dash Original Seasoning

2-1/2 cups fusilli pasta (Catelli)

4-6 multigrain buns

shorts...
access to cold water...

<u>**Serves 4-6**</u>

15 Eating Time

(from when you get home from work)

Equipment List:

...the night before...
Crockpot
Cutting board
Sharp meat knife
Sharp veggie knife
Lge mixing spoon
Measuring cups & spoons

...when you get home...
Measuring cups

Per serving:

Calories	320
Fat	6.2 g
Protein	26.6 g
Carbohydrate	39.5 g

Food Choices:

2	Starch
1/2	Fruits + Veg
0	Milk 1%
1/2	Sugars
3	Protein
0	Fat
0	Extras

Prep Time

Chicken Noodle Soup

4

Beef Chow Mein Stir-Fry with Rice

Instructions:

Don't change yet! Take out equipment.
1. Combine rice and water in a large microwave-safe pot or casserole with lid. <u>Cover</u> and **microwave** at high 10 minutes, then medium 10 minutes.

2. Heat oil in a large nonstick fry pan or wok at med-high.
   Cut steak into thin strips and add to pan as you cut.
   Chop onion into large wedges and slice mushrooms adding to meat pan as you cut.

   Rinse vegetables in a colander and add to meat pan stirring until mixed.
   Add to pan in this order; brown sugar, soy sauce and oyster sauce.

   <u>Simmer</u> until timer rings for the rice.

   ...when timer rings for rice...
   Toss the bean sprouts into the chow mein pan and stir.

3. Let rice stand for 5 minutes to set. When rice is ready so is the beef chow mein.

Tip
If it's a really hot day you can do step 2 in a foil wrap or bag (see page 3), but double wrap so the sauce doesn't leak.
* Remember to add the bean sprouts at the end, reclosing the wrap to let them steam for a few minutes while the rice is setting.

Ingredients:

Take out ingredients.
1-1/2 cups basmati or white rice
3 cups water

1 tsp canola oil

1.5 lbs or 675 g lean sirloin steak

1 onion
7-10 mushrooms

2 cups oriental style frozen vegetables
2 Tbsp <u>each</u> of <u>brown sugar</u> and <u>soy sauce</u> (V-H)
4 Tbsp oyster sauce

1 cup fresh bean sprouts
1/2-1 tsp chili flakes *if you like things spicy*

Optional *Ron and the kids love crunchy chow mein noodles sprinkled on top after it's served.*

<u>**Serves 4-6**</u>

30 Eating Time

Equipment List:

Lge microwave-safe pot
Lge nonstick fry pan or wok
  (or 2 large pieces of foil)
Colander
Sharp meat knife
Sharp veggie knife
Lge mixing spoon
Measuring cups
Measuring spoons

Per serving:

Calories	357
Fat	6.5 g
Protein	31.0 g
Carbohydrate	43.7 g

Food Choices:

2	Starch
1/2	Fruits + Veg
0	Milk 1%
1	Sugars
4	Protein
1/2	Fat
0	Extras

Prep Time

Beef Chow Mein

4

Italian Baked Chicken with Garlic Fusilli and Vegetables

Instructions:

Don't change yet! Take out equipment.

1. <u>Preheat BBQ</u> to med (approx 350° F).
   Place chicken in a large oven-safe cake pan or casserole dish.
   Sprinkle with spice and brown sugar.

   Drain mushrooms and scatter over each thigh.
   Cover <u>each</u> thigh with pasta sauce one spoon at a time using the whole jar.

   Place pan on foil diffuser (see page 3) in **preheated BBQ**. <u>Close lid</u>.
   Set timer for 35 minutes.

2. Prepare dip and **refrigerate**.

   Wash and cut up fresh veggies to eat raw.

3. Fill a large **stove-top** pot with water.
   Let stand.
   When the timer rings for the chicken, <u>turn the BBQ to low and leave the chicken in the BBQ</u>.
   Bring water for pasta to a boil.
   Add pasta to boiling water. Set timer for 7 minutes. Stir occasionally.
   Rinse pasta in a colander under hot water when the timer rings. Return to pot <u>no heat</u> and toss with a little olive oil if you wish.

Ingredients:

Take out ingredients.

8-12 boneless skinless chicken thighs (1-3/4 lbs or 800 grams)
1 tsp Mrs. Dash Italian Seasoning for all
3 Tbsp brown sugar for all

1 can (10 oz or 284 mL) sliced mushrooms
1 jar (24.5 oz or 700 mL) Catelli Garden Select pasta sauce *Parmesan & Romano*

aluminum foil (Alcan)

1/2 cup veggie dip
(see back cover or use bottled)

2 large carrots
2 celery stalks
4 broccoli florets

water

3-3/4 cups Catelli Bistro fusilli pasta *Garlic & Parsley*

1 tsp olive oil (optional)
Parmesan cheese (optional, but soooo delicious sprinkled on the chicken)

Note *Use deboned thighs only (as a shorter cooking time is best to keep these saucy).*

<u>**Serves 4-6**</u>

60 Eating Time

Equipment List:

BBQ
BBQ tongs
Lge oven-safe cake pan or
   casserole dish
Lge stove-top pot
Small bowl for dip
Colander
Spoon
Teaspoon
Measuring spoons

Per serving:

Calories	525
Fat	9.4 g
Protein	41.1 g
Carbohydrate	69.1 g

Food Choices:

3	Starch
1 1/2	Fruits + Veg
0	Milk 1%
1	Sugars
4 1/2	Protein
1/2	Fat
0	Extras

Prep Time

Italian Baked Chicken

Things You Should Know
About the Recipes

Yellow

This is a perfect meal for those cloudy days because it's soooo fast! If you want to make this a veggie version, omit the meat and toss in firm tofu. Deeelicious!

Green

The test families love this "I cook, you clean" meal. Caution! You must make sure your BBQ is preheated before baking the corn muffins. Also use the heavy-duty foil for your diffuser (see page 3) or you'll burn the bottoms. Check often. To make the veggie version use the veggie grind.

Red Wings

Ron prefers to use the cooked chicken roasters for this meal. Either way this is a fun, easy meal with great nutritional data... bet ya never thought about cooking fries on the BBQ, now did ya???

Yellow

These are really different and just amazing! It's sort of a feel good meal for summer! Remember to get family members involved with the prep...it changes the dynamics of suppertime...you'll see!

Blue

If you make the BBQ sauce on the back flap, you may never buy BBQ sauce again. You can always double the BBQ sauce recipe, as it stores well in the refrigerator.

Week 5

Yellow: Szechuan Orange-Ginger Chicken
with Pasta and Vegetables

Our Family Rating: 10
Your Family Rating: _____

Green: Beef Barley Soup with BBQ
Corn Muffins

Our Family Rating: 9
Your Family Rating: _____

Red Wings: Hot Turkey Sandwiches with
French Fries and Peas

Our Family Rating: 8.5
Your Family Rating: _____

Yellow: Spanish Meat Patties with Rice
and Vegetable Skillet

Our Family Rating: 8.5
Your Family Rating: _____

Blue: BBQ Chicken with Green Leaf Salad

Our Family Rating: 10
Your Family Rating: _____

5

Szechuan Orange-Ginger Chicken with Pasta and Vegetables

Instructions:

Don't change yet! Take out equipment.

1. Bring water to a boil in a large **stove-top** pot <u>with lid</u> at high.

2. Heat oil in a large nonstick fry pan or wok at med-high.
   Cut chicken into bite size pieces and gradually add to pan as you cut. Stir until meat is no longer pink.
   Combine in this order, in a small bowl; tahini, dry-garlic sauce, sherry, orange juice, cumin, brown sugar, ginger, garlic and chili sauce.

   Stir together and pour over chicken.

   Stir and **lower heat** to a high simmer.

   Sliver red pepper and add to chicken. Stir.

3. Rinse vegetables in a colander under cold water. Place in a medium size microwave-safe pot or casserole dish <u>with lid</u>.
   Microwave at high for 5 minutes, then let stand.

4. Place pasta in boiling water and set timer for 4-6 minutes.

5. Add spice to vegetables and **microwave** at high for 2 additional minutes <u>just before serving</u>.

   The sauce is meant to be poured over the individual servings of pasta. My family looove this dish with crunchy chow mein noodles and peanuts scattered on top!!!

Ingredients:

Take out ingredients.

1 tsp canola or olive oil

3 boneless skinless chicken breasts (approx 1 lb or 450 g)

2 Tbsp tahini (*ground sesame seeds, looks like peanut butter*)
1/4 cup V-H dry-garlic sauce
1/4 cup sherry (*or...add 1/4 cup red wine w/ 1-1/2 tsp brown sugar*)
1/2 cup orange juice (McCain)
1 tsp ground cumin
2 tsp <u>each</u> of <u>brown sugar, ground ginger, prepared garlic</u> and <u>bottled hot chili sauce</u>
If you like it really spicy add more chili sauce.

1/2 red pepper (or 1 small)
4 cups cut frozen broccoli

3/4 lb or 350 g vermicelli pasta (Catelli)

1 tsp Mrs. Dash Original Seasoning
butter or margarine (optional)

chow mein noodles (optional)
salted peanuts (optional)

<u>Serves 4-6</u>

  30 Eating Time

Equipment List:

Lge nonstick fry pan or
  wok
Lge stove-top pot w/lid
Microwave-safe pot w/lid
Colander
Small mixing bowl
Cutting board
Sharp veggie knife
Sharp meat knife
Pasta fork
Lge & small mixing spoons
Measuring cups & spoons

Per serving:

Calories	387
Fat	5.3 g
Protein	27.7 g
Carbohydrate	57.0 g

Food Choices:

3	Starch
1/2	Fruits + Veg
0	Milk 1%
1	Sugars
3	Protein
1	Fat
0	Extras

Prep Time

Szechuan Orange-Ginger Chicken

Beef Barley Soup with BBQ Corn Muffins

Instructions:

...the night before...
Take out equipment.
1. Brown meat in a large non-stick pan at med-high until meat is no longer red.
   ...while meat is browning...
Chop onion and celery in that order and add to meat pan as you cut. Stir to combine. Toss into the centre crock of the **crockpot**.

Add the following in this order; tomato soup, consommé, water, diced tomatoes, carrots, bay leaf, pepper, seasoning and barley.

Stir to combine and store in the **fridge** overnight.

...in the morning...
Return center pot <u>with cover</u> to the outer crock and set on **low heat**.

...when you get home for supper...
2. **Preheat BBQ** to med (approx 350° F).

Combine flour, sugar, cornmeal and baking powder in a mixing bowl.

Combine oil, milk, and egg in a measuring cup and blend with a fork. <u>Add liquid ingredients to dry ingredients</u> and stir with fork until mixed. Distribute evenly into sprayed muffin tins 1/2 full (approx 8). Place on foil diffuser (see page 3) in **preheated BBQ**. <u>Close lid</u>.
Set timer for 10-12 minutes checking that temperature stays stable. When toothpick comes clean they're done.

Ingredients:

...the night before...
Take out ingredients.
1 lb or 450 g ground beef (90% lean)

1 onion
2 celery stalks

1 can (10 oz or 284 mL) <u>each</u> of <u>tomato soup</u> and <u>consommé</u>
2 soup cans filled with water
1 can (14 oz or 398 mL) diced tomatoes
2 cups frozen baby carrots
1 bay leaf
1/4 tsp fresh ground pepper
2 tsp Mrs. Dash Italian Seasoning
1/4 cup pot barley
If you like things spicy add hot chili sauce.

1 cup flour
1/4 cup white sugar
3/4 cup cornmeal
1 Tbsp baking powder

1/4 cup canola oil
3/4 cup 1% milk
1 egg

cooking spray (PAM)
aluminum foil (Alcan)

<u>Serves 4-6</u>

 Eating Time

(from when you get home from work)

Equipment List:

...the night before...
Crockpot
Lge nonstick fry pan
Cutting board
Can opener
Sharp veggie knife
Lge mixing spoon
Measuring cups & spoons

...when you get home...
BBQ
Muffin tin, shiny metal best
Large mixing bowl
Mixing spoon & fork
Measuring cups

Per serving:

Calories	550
Fat	23.8 g
Protein	25.2 g
Carbohydrate	58.7 g

Food Choices:

2	Starch
1 1/2	Fruits + Veg
0	Milk 1%
1 1/2	Sugars
2 1/2	Protein
3 1/2	Fat
0	Extras

Prep Time

Beef Barley Soup

Hot Turkey Sandwiches with French Fries and Peas

Instructions:

Don't change yet! Take out equipment.
1. <u>Preheat BBQ</u> to med (approx 350° F).

2. Rinse peas under cold water in a colander.
   Place in microwave-safe pot and
   microwave at high for 5 minutes.
   Let stand.

3. Spray a large cake pan with cooking spray.
   Add a layer of French fries and spray again.
   Place in **preheated BBQ**. <u>Close lid</u>.
   Set timer for 5 minutes.

   Prepare gravy mix according to package
   directions in a small **stove-top** pot.

   ...when timer rings...
   Flip fries and reset timer for 4 minutes.

4. **Microwave** sliced turkey for 2-3 minutes
   or until warm.

5. Stir peas and cook an additional 1 minute.

   ...when timer rings for fries...
   ...it's ready to serve.
6. Place bread directly on serving plates.

   Place sliced turkey on bread and top
   with gravy and pepper.

Option
*Ron loves to use a precooked roasting
chicken for this meal instead of deli meat.
This is a perfect time to get kids making a
chicken salad with part of the leftover roaster,
while you are making supper, ...then you have
a lunch done too!*

Ingredients:

Take out ingredients.

2 cups frozen baby peas

cooking spray (PAM)
1 lb or 450 g French fries
(McCain SuperQuick 5 min fries)

1 pkg dry gravy mix (for poultry)
(approx 30 g)

3/4 lb or 350 g sliced deli turkey
or chicken

6-8 slices whole wheat bread

fresh ground pepper to taste

*This is an easy feel-good meal
without the summer heat!*

<u>**Serves 4-6**</u>

25 Eating Time

Equipment List:

BBQ
Small stove-top pot
Microwave-safe pot w/lid
Lge cake pan
Colander
Spatula
Mixing spoons
Fork

Per serving:

Calories	393
Fat	13.3 g
Protein	25.9 g
Carbohydrate	42.4 g

Food Choices:

2	Starch
1/2	Fruits + Veg
0	Milk 1%
1/2	Sugars
3	Protein
2	Fat
0	Extras

Prep Time

Hot Turkey Sandwiches

Spanish Meat Patties with Rice and Vegetable Skillet

Instructions:

Don't change yet! Take out equipment.
1. <u>Preheat BBQ</u> to med (approx 350° F).

2. Combine rice and water in a large microwave-safe pot or casserole <u>with lid</u>. **Microwave** according to pkg directions.

3. Combine the following in a large bowl in this order; ground beef, cornflake crumbs, salsa, onion flakes, spices and garlic.

   Form into 4-6 large patties and **grill** on **BBQ**. <u>Close lid</u>.
   Cook each side 5-10 minutes or until center is well cooked.

   ...meanwhile...

4. Spray a large piece of foil, shiny side in, with cooking spray.
   Coarsely chop onion and tomatoes and slice mushrooms. Heap in centre of foil as you cut. Sprinkle with spice, drizzle with oil and wrap (see page 3).
   Place on **BBQ** beside meat (approx 5-7 minutes <u>turning once</u>). <u>Close lid</u>.

5. Place cooked meat in a serving dish <u>with lid</u> until veggies are cooked.

   In a small **stove-top** pot combine ketchup, broth and spices. Heat and stir until well blended. Remove from heat.

   Warm patties in the **microwave** for 2 min.

   Serve patties on the rice with veggies on the side. Pour sauce on top of each patty.

Ingredients:

Take out ingredients.

1 or 2 pkgs mushroom or garden vegetable flavored rice (6 oz or 165 g / pkg)

1-1/2 lbs or 675 g ground beef (90% lean)
1/4 cup cornflake crumbs *usually found in coating mix section*
1/4 cup chunky salsa
2 tsp onion flakes
1 tsp <u>each</u> of <u>Mrs. Dash Italian Seasoning</u> and <u>prepared garlic</u>
fresh ground pepper to taste

aluminum foil (Alcan)
cooking spray (PAM)
1 onion
2 tomatoes
15 mushrooms
1 tsp <u>each</u> of <u>salt</u>, <u>rosemary</u>, <u>dried parsley</u> and <u>extra virgin olive oil</u>

1 cup hot ketchup
1/2 cup beef broth (I freeze the rest)
1/2 tsp Mrs. Dash Italian Seasoning
fresh ground pepper to taste

Option *Black olives not only taste great with this, but have an amazing presentation.*

<u>Serves 4-6</u>

(30) Eating Time

Equipment List:

BBQ
BBQ spatula
Small stove-top pot
Lge microwave-safe pot
  w/lid
Lge mixing bowl
Serving dish w/lid
Cutting board
Mixing spoon
Sharp veggie knife
Measuring cups and spoons

Per serving:

Calories	441
Fat	19.4 g
Protein	26.1 g
Carbohydrate	40.4 g

Food Choices:

1 1/2	Starch
1/2	Fruits + Veg
0	Milk 1%
1	Sugars
3 1/2	Protein
2	Fat
0	Extras

Prep Time

Spanish Meat Patties

BBQ Chicken with Green Leaf Salad

Instructions:

Don't change yet! Take out equipment.
1. <u>Preheat BBQ</u> to med (approx 350° F).

   Prepare BBQ sauce from back cover or use your favorite bottled sauce.

   Unroll chicken thighs and lightly spray each piece with cooking spray <u>before</u> you **grill** on **BBQ**.
   Brush the tops with BBQ sauce. <u>Close lid</u>.
   Set timer for 10 minutes. Check often but don't flip until well seared.

2. Tear lettuce into bite size pieces into the salad spinner. Rinse under cold water and spin dry. Transfer to salad bowl.

   Prepare poppyseed dressing and pour over lettuce as desired. Toss to coat.
   Divide onto individual serving plates.

   Sprinkle with bacon bits and croutons if you wish.

   Cut oranges into slices or segments and place on salad for a fresh summer look.

   ...when timer rings...
3. Turn chicken over and brush with remaining BBQ sauce.
   Set timer for 10 minutes. Check often.

4. Serve with your favorite buns.

   When timer rings again, supper is ready!

Ingredients:

Take out ingredients.

1/2 cup BBQ sauce (use bottled or see back cover)

8-12 boneless skinless chicken thighs (1-3/4 lb or 800 g) cooking spray (PAM)
Note   If you are using larger thighs with bone in this will take longer to cook.

1 large head green leaf lettuce

1/2 cup poppyseed dressing (see back cover or use bottled)

bacon bits (optional)
croutons (optional)

2 oranges

4-6 whole wheat buns
or...if your family want a heartier meal replace buns with rice or potatoes

<u>Serves 4-6</u>

  Eating Time

Equipment List:

BBQ
BBQ tools
Salad spinner
2 small mixing bowls
Serving dish w/ lid (for
  chicken)
Cutting board
Mixing spoons
Sharp veggie knife
Measuring cups & spoons

Per serving:

Calories	324
Fat	8.5 g
Protein	32.1 g
Carbohydrate	29.8 g

Food Choices:

1	Starch
1/2	Fruits + Veg
0	Milk 1%
1	Sugars
4	Protein
1/2	Fat
0	Extras

Prep Time

BBQ Chicken

5

Write your own recipe reading left to right.

Prep Time

Instructions:

Don't change yet! Take out equipment.

Ingredients:

Take out ingredients.

Eating Time

Write your own recipe reading left to right.

Instructions:

Don't change yet! Take out equipment.

Ingredients:

Take out ingredients.

  Eating Time

Write your own recipe reading left to right.

Prep Time

Instructions:

Don't change yet! Take out equipment.

Ingredients:

Take out ingredients.

Eating Time

Magnetic Wallets

I swear our wallets start to vibrate the minute one of our kids walk by!!!

...which has very little to do with what I have to say.
I just needed to share that with the cooking population.

Thank you for listening.

Stress Free Meal Plans

(Yea right!!!)   **No, Really!!**

Remember when I mentioned earlier that 85% of North Americans have no idea what they are having for supper…until supper?

I would like to walk you through how I used to do my meal plans and why it didn't work. I wonder if anyone can relate!

I would decide, "This week I am going to be very organized." I would write down the five meals I was going to have in my workweek. I would haul out the recipes and go around the kitchen deciding what I had and what I didn't have. As I came across the items I didn't have, I would write them on a list. (Or I would even sometimes circle them on those snazzy little premade lists with a million items on them. You know the ones where the writing is so small, I'm sure they were made for elves.) I am now left with a list of, let's say, 14 items. I go to the store with the list of the items I will need and include things like shampoos, etc… I feel fantastic! My grocery bill is actually affordable. I make the meals on the plan that week and my whole life, home and relationships seem calmer, nicer!

I swear I am going to do this again next week...which I may or may not do...depending on the demands of my job...ooor soccer, hockey, dancing, swimming, piano, basketball, band, karate or gumg-go lessons...Ok, I made the last one up...but I'm sure they'll invent something like that soon... just to make my kids feel like they're missing out on something!

What was my problem?

I was not only eating backwards, **I was meal planning backwards** as well! It dawned on me that my meal planning stay power lasted about three weeks. That's when martyrdom set in...this is when I started feeling sorry for myself. "Why should I always be the one to think about planning supper?"

I was stressed out! You can climb over the laundry heap...but **you can't ignore eating**! It's the thing you can't put off until tomorrow. It's the one thing you must do! The food industry knows this! Again, it is **no accident that grocery stores are constantly increasing their space for prepackaged supper in a box**. It's also no accident that there is a fast food joint going up on every corner every time we turn around.

Food manufacturers are profiting on our emotions baby...and we're letting them do it! We're stressed out and **we impulse buy** all because we believe meal planning is hard. Of course we want food manufacturers to make a profit so our economy is strong...we just want to **make sure we are in control of our health**, not them!

If you examine the first three grocery lists on pages 102, 103 and 104 you will clearly **see where our problem lies**. One way you end up with **14 items and a useless piece of paper**, which you will throw away. The other you end up with the **same 14 items**, taken from an original complete meal plan, **which you will always have**. When you don't have the energy to meal plan the next time...you **use a copy of one you've already created**. When you do have energy...you will simply be adding to your library of meal plans.

You have no idea the difference this will make in your life!

Read on, if you really want to fix this.

Let's talk about the martyrdom part. Here's how I explain it in a nutshell. Ron almost always takes out the garbage in our home…I almost always think about what we are having for supper. Find something your partner almost always does and if you're the one who thinks about supper…quit your complaining and include them in a stress free way. Who doesn't want to have input in what they're eating during the high stress workweek? We all do!!! The part the noncook, nonplanner doesn't like, is a person phoning them at work saying, "What do you want for supper?" This person knows that this is a loaded question. The answer under pressure is usually, "I don't know." The cook-planner inevitably will then slip into the ever grumpy martyrdom mode! Buuuuut…if you really think about it, you wouldn't be calling if you knew what you were having for supper yourself, now would you?

Sooooo, it's the thinking you want help with!

We all know that under pressure no one is thinking clearly…everyone is just stressed out from the demand of his or her jobs. (…and if someone is at home as a fulltime care giver, believe me…the job is extremely draining and demanding!)

I suggest this… **If you are the supper-planner-thinker** in your home right now, **it's going to be your job** to turn this into a stress free experience. You can **either keep going the hard way**, so you feel sad, depressed and angry, **or you can do it an easy way**, so you feel great and more connected with your family! Your choice!!!

Because our summer book is a smaller size than our core book, Life's on Fire - Cooking for the Rushed, the grocery lists are smaller in size. If you plan on making a commitment to give this a try…you may want to **download our larger size grocery lists** from our website; **www.cookingfortherushed.com** or write directly on the blank lists at the back of Life's On Fire - Cooking for the Rushed. This way you always know where those lists are. You can use the blanks in this book as well, you will simply need to write quite small.

The following steps will change everything!

Meal Planning Steps

Start the changes in your eating life.

1. **Explain** to your family you are going to stop complaining about supper and make a few **easy changes** that will **add peace** to your home. Tell them **you need them to get involved** for a few minutes each week.

2. Present them with a **blank grocery list** and ask them to help **choose meals** they love. (If it's hot dogs and fries…you have to give in sometimes.) See our example grocery lists. As the family pick, you will have to say yes or no depending on how the week is shaping up as far as being **nutritionally balanced**. For example…if everyone that week wants chicken and rice, it just won't work. You will have to get someone to pick his or her second choice.

3. Now that you have the **names of five meals** written on the blanks at the top of the grocery list…get the family to help **pull out the recipe books** these meals belong to. They are to put those books in front of you with the pages bookmarked. Thank them for their help and tell them that **you will do the rest**. Just watch the looks on their faces as they walk away in shock that you are completely in control…without a scowl on your face! They will think you've lost it!!

4. Make out your **grocery list** as if you are doing it **for a friend**. Do not go look to see what you have and what you do not have in the house for groceries. **List all of the groceries** in the appropriate categories. (If you are using a book where the recipes are only one-component recipes…don't forget to add to your list the components you usually serve with it.)

You got this far. Way to go!

Meal Planning Steps (Cont.)

5. After you are done…look at your list and walk through your pantry, fridge and freezer…**deciding what you don't have on that list**. **Write those items** as you come across them on a **blank sheet of paper**. (You only have to use a blank sheet of paper in combination with your complete list when you create a new meal plan.)

6. Take your **blank sheet** of paper with you to do **groceries the first time** and later in the week **make five copies of your complete list**.

    The **best success** we hear about, is when people **write directly on the blank lists in the back of <u>Life's on Fire</u>**. This way you always know where your complete lists are. **Store your photocopies** in the front and back pockets of the book. If you do not have a copy of <u>Life's on Fire</u>, we suggest you purchase a thin binder, plastic sheet covers and a hole punch. Place your complete list in the plastic cover with the hole-punched copies behind it in the binder. The **savings on your grocery bill** will pay for these items in no time.

7. The last and final step is to **decide what you will be serving** the following evening, according to your schedule. Take meat out to **defrost if necessary** and most important…**share your information**!!! Let people know what you're having. **Leave the recipe out** on the kitchen counter. **Ask someone** in the family **to take out** the **equipment** and the **groceries** after school or work the following day to help speed up the meal making process. (The exceptions are things that need to stay in the fridge.) If I get **home at the same time** as the person I've asked, it turns into a one on one time as we **do it together**.

Once you remove the stress from the supper hour you just may have time for that walk after all.

If nothing else;

Your whole family's dynamics will change in relation to this very stressful time of day!!!

G R O C E R Y L I S T S

These are your grocery lists. Remember...never tear them out! Photocopy them and store a few copies of each in the front or back pocket.

Ooooooor......

Customize your own lists...using recipes you want to try from our book, in combination with recipes you already have and trust. Follow steps 4, 5 and 6 on pages 99 and 100. Then photocopy and store your own lists.

Either way... It's all ready for you to

Get Started!

What we usually do is write
down only what we need.

Grocery List

Hog Town Pizza
Darling Beef
Beef Enchilada Casserole
Honey-Mustard Chicken Burgers
Karen's Chicken

1-1/2 lbs or 675 g lean sirloin steak
4 large boneless skinless chicken breasts 1-1/2 lbs or 700 g
gruyere cheese - 1 cup grated
pizza crusts 2
green leaf lettuce 1 bunch
cantaloupe
strawberries 8
Roma tomatoes 3+4+2 optional
12 oven ready lasagna noodles
onion flakes
liquid honey
artichokes (canned)
soy sauce
4-6 multigrain hamburger buns

How will this help you when you
want to repeat this plan?

Complete Grocery List - Master

Complete meal plan ready to photocopy

Custom Grocery List

Recipe Name	Page #
Hog Town Pizza (Life's On Fire)	160
Darling Beef (Mom's Church Book)	121
Beef Enchilada Casserole (Life's On Fire)	34
Honey-Mustard Chicken B (Getting Ya...)	36
Karen's Chicken (Recipe File)	

Meats

1-1/2 lbs or 675 g lean sirloin steak
1-1/2 lbs or 675 g ground beef (90% lean)
4 large boneless skinless chicken breasts
   1-1/2 lbs or 700 g
8-12 boneless skinless chicken thighs
   2 lbs or 900 g
16 thin slices deli salami 50 g

Dairy

gruyere cheese, 1 cup grated
pizza crusts 2
Cheddar cheese, 1 cup grated
part-skim mozza, 1 cup grated
French vanilla yogourt, low-fat
butter

Produce

prepared garlic (in a jar)
green onions 4+2
Roma tomatoes 3+4+2 optional
green leaf lettuce 1 bunch
small onion 1+1 optional
potatoes large 4
avocados 2
cantaloupe
red or green grapes
strawberries 8

Other

aluminum foil

Spices

basil
thyme
rosemary
oregano
onion flakes
lemon pepper
Mrs. Dash Italian Seasoning
Mrs. Dash Extra Spicy Seasoning
salt and pepper

Baking Goods

balsamic vinegar
brown sugar
cooking spray
olive oil
gravy mix, dry

Helpers

beef broth
1 can chopped green chilies
1 can Cheddar cheese soup
1 can artichokes
chunky salsa
Dijon mustard
soy sauce
Worcestershire sauce
liquid honey
mayonnaise (optional)

Frozen Food

broccoli
peas and carrots

Baking

4-6 multigrain hamburger buns

Dry Essentials

12 oven ready lasagna noodles
1-1/2 cups white rice
croutons (optional)

You will always have this complete plan to use again.

Items you have on hand are crossed out on a
photocopy of your master complete grocery list.

Custom Grocery List

Recipe Name   Page
Hog Town Pizza (Life's On Fire)   160
Darling Beef (Mom's Church Book)   121
Beef Enchilada Casserole (Life's On Fire)   34
Honey-Mustard Chicken B (Getting Ya...)   36
Karen's Chicken (Recipe File)

Meats
1-1/2 lbs or 675 g lean sirloin steak
~~1-1/2 lbs or 675 g ground beef (90% lean)~~
4 large boneless skinless chicken breasts
   1-1/2 lbs or 700 g
~~8-12 boneless skinless chicken thighs~~
   ~~2 lbs or 900 g~~
~~16 thin slices deli salami 50 g~~

Dairy
gruyere cheese, 1 cup grated
pizza crusts 2
~~Cheddar cheese, 1 cup grated~~
~~part skim mozza, 1 cup grated~~
~~French vanilla yogourt, low fat~~
~~butter~~

Produce
~~prepared garlic (in a jar)~~
~~green onions 4+2~~
Roma tomatoes 3+4+2 optional
green leaf lettuce 1 bunch
~~small onion 1+1 optional~~
~~potatoes large 4~~
~~avocados 2~~
cantaloupe
~~red or green grapes~~
strawberries 8

Other
~~aluminum foil~~

Spices
~~basil~~
~~thyme~~
~~rosemary~~
~~oregano~~
onion flakes
~~lemon pepper~~
~~Mrs. Dash Italian Seasoning~~
~~Mrs. Dash Extra Spicy Seasoning~~
~~salt and pepper~~

Baking Goods
~~balsamic vinegar~~
~~brown sugar~~
~~cooking spray~~
~~olive oil~~
~~gravy mix, dry~~

Helpers
~~beef broth~~
~~1 can chopped green chilies~~
~~1 can Cheddar cheese soup~~
1 can artichokes
~~chunky salsa~~
~~Dijon mustard~~
soy sauce
~~Worcestershire sauce~~
liquid honey
~~mayonnaise (optional)~~

Frozen Food
~~broccoli~~
~~peas and carrots~~

Baking
4-6 multigrain hamburger buns

Dry Essentials
12 oven ready lasagna noodles
~~1-1/2 cups white rice~~
~~croutons (optional)~~

You still end up with the same 14 items.
The difference is you have the original plan
and will never have to recreate it again.

Recipe Name	Page #
Plum Chicken	34
Honey-Mustard Chicken Burgers	36
BBQ Style Beef	38
Cajun Chicken-Caesar Salad	40
Beef & Broccoli	42

Meats

real prepared bacon bits (optional)
precooked roaster chicken 2.2 lbs or 1 kg
  (you will only use 1/2, extra for lunch)
10-12 boneless skinless chicken thighs
  (1-3/4 lbs or 800 g)
4 large boneless skinless chicken breasts
  (1-1/2 lbs or 700 g)
lean sirloin beef (3-1/2 lbs or 1.575 kg)

Dairy

Parmesan cheese, grated low-fat
1 cup French vanilla yogurt (low-fat)

Produce

prepared garlic (in a jar)
1 lge bunch Romaine lettuce
  (more if using on chicken burgers)
3 onions (1 optional)
1-1/2 green peppers
4-6 large potatoes
4 med size tomatoes (2 optional)
16 stalks asparagus (3/4 lb or 340 g)
10-12 mushrooms
3 florets broccoli
1 small zucchini
1/2 cantaloupe or melon (3/4 lb or 350 g)
1 bunch red or green grapes
  (3/4 lb or 350 g)
8 strawberries
2 small kiwi
precooked vermicelli noodles 1 lb or 450 g

Dry Essentials

croutons
1-1/2 cups white or brown rice

Bakery

8-12 multigrain buns (2 meals)

Spices

basil leaves
chili flakes
cumin
curry powder
garlic powder
ginger powder
Mrs. Dash Extra Spicy Seasoning
Mrs. Dash Italian Seasoning
Mrs. Dash Peppercorn Blend
paprika
salt & pepper

Baking Goods

canola oil
cooking spray (PAM)
olive oil, extra-virgin
brown sugar
cornstarch
flour
lemon juice
red wine vinegar

Helpers

1 can corn (14 oz or 398 mL)
chicken broth, 1/4 cup
ketchup
BBQ sauce (or see back cover)
Dijon mustard
mayonnaise, lowest-fat
salad dressing, gourmet Caesar
soy sauce (V-H)
plum sauce (V-H)
dry-garlic sauce (V-H)
hoisin sauce
chili sauce, hot (bottled)
ginger-sesame-Thai sauce
liquid honey
peach jam

Other

aluminum foil (Alcan), reg & heavy duty

Custom Grocery List

Recipe Names   **Page #**

_____

_____

_____

_____

_____

Meats

Dairy

Produce

Dry Essentials

Spices

Baking Goods

Helpers

Frozen Food

Bakery

Other

Meats

real prepared bacon bits (optional)
4-6 thin slices deli cooked ham
   (7 oz or 200 g)
boneless trimmed pork chops 1 lb or 450 g
   (or boneless skinless chicken)
4 large boneless skinless chicken breasts
   (1-1/2 lbs or 675 g)
lean sirloin beef (3-1/2 lbs or 1.6 kg)

Dairy

2 cups grated mozza cheese, part-skim
Parmesan cheese, grated low-fat
1% milk
butter
sour cream, no-fat (optional)

Produce

prepared garlic (in a jar)
3 onions
15 pearl onions (or 2 small)
4-6 large potatoes
1 small zucchini
31-33 mushrooms
1 red pepper
3 green peppers
1 bag baby spinach leaves 10 oz or 284 g
green onion (optional)
6 strawberries

Dry Essentials

1-1/2 cups white rice
1-1/2 cups whole wheat couscous (quick)

Bakery

2   12" bakery pizza crusts
fine bread crumbs
4-6 slices whole wheat bread

Spices

bay leaf
celery salt
chili flakes (optional)
curry powder
garlic powder
ginger powder
Mrs. Dash Italian Seasoning
Mrs. Dash Original Seasoning
paprika
parsley, dried
salt & pepper

Baking Goods

brown sugar
canola oil
cooking spray (PAM)
cornstarch
vinegar

Helpers

1 cup Catelli pizza sauce (Spicy Garlic &
   Onion for more zip)
tomato paste
3 Tbsp prepared basil pesto (in a jar)
tahini (ground sesame seeds-looks like
   peanut butter)
mayonnaise, lowest-fat
poppyseed dressing (or see back cover)
soy sauce (V-H)
1 can beef broth (10 oz or 284 mL)
1 can cream of mushroom soup
   (10 oz or 284 mL)
1 can unsweetened pineapple slices
   (14 oz or 398 mL)

Frozen Food

4 cups broccoli
spinach, chopped (4 oz or 115 g)

Other

aluminum foil (Alcan), reg & heavy duty
3 Tbsp brandy
1 cup sherry (or red wine)

Custom Grocery List

Recipe Names   **Page #**

_____

_____

_____

_____

_____

Meats

Dairy

Produce

Dry Essentials

Spices

Baking Goods

Helpers

Frozen Food

Bakery

Other

Meats

4 lge boneless skinless chicken breasts
   (1-1/2 lbs or 675 g)
10-12 boneless skinless chicken thighs
   (1-3/4 lbs or 800 g)
12 thin slices deli roasted lean beef
   (1/2 lb or 225 g)
lean pork or beef ribs (3 lbs or 1350 g)

Dairy

Parmesan cheese, grated low-fat (optional)
1/2 cup grated mozza cheese, part-skim
4-5 cups cheese tortellini
butter

Produce

prepared garlic (in a jar)
2 onions
1 spaghetti squash (2.2 lbs or 1 kg)
   (or potatoes)
3 lge celery stalks
1 lge carrot
1/2 English cucumber
1 bunch green leaf or Romaine lettuce
1 bag baby spinach leaves 10 oz or 284 g
2 green onions
1 cup bean sprouts (optional)
1 red pepper
16 stalks of asparagus (3/4 lb or 340 g)
10 mushrooms
4-6 corn on the cob

Dry Essentials

1-1/2 cups basmati rice
whole wheat crackers (optional)

Other

bamboo skewers
1/2 cup light beer (can be nonalcoholic)
aluminum foil (Alcan), reg & heavy duty

Spices

bayleaf
cayenne pepper
chili flakes
chili powder
cumin powder
curry powder
garlic powder
Mrs. Dash Garlic & Herb Seasoning
Mrs. Dash Italian Seasoning
onion flakes
parsley, dried
salt & pepper

Baking Goods

brown sugar
canola oil
cooking spray (PAM)
olive oil, extra-virgin
cider vinegar

Helpers

1 jar Catelli Garden Select pasta sauce
   Country Mushroom (24.5 oz or 700 mL)
chicken broth, 1 lge tetrapak
   (30 oz or 900 mL)
1 can tomato soup (10 oz or 284 mL)
1 can sliced mushrooms (10 oz or 284 mL)
salad dressing, sundried tomato & oregano
honey-mustard dressing (or see back cover)
soy sauce (V-H)
Worcestershire sauce
ketchup
chili sauce, hot (bottled)
chunky salsa
peanut butter, creamy low-fat

Frozen Food

2 cups mixed veggies

Bakery

1 baguette or French loaf
4-6 multigrain buns

Custom Grocery List

Recipe Names   **Page #**

_____

_____

_____

_____

_____

Meats

Dairy

Produce

Dry Essentials

Spices

Baking Goods

Helpers

Frozen Food

Bakery

Other

Recipe Names   Page

Meats

precooked roaster chicken 2.2 lbs or 1 kg
   (available in deli)
8-12 boneless skinless chicken thighs
   (1-3/4 lbs or 800 g)
beef sirloin roast (1-1/2 lbs or 675 g)
lean sirloin steak (1-1/2 lbs or 675 g)

Dairy

sour cream, no-fat
Parmesan cheese, grated low-fat (optional)

Produce

prepared garlic (in a jar)
veggie dip (or see back cover)
4-6 large potatoes
3 onions
4 stalks celery
4 large carrots
1 head broccoli
7-10 mushrooms
1 cup bean sprouts
1 lge bunch green leaf or butter lettuce
1 large ripe avocado
red seedless grapes (1/2 lb or 225 g)
2 oranges or mandarins (optional)

Dry Essentials

3-3/4 cups Catelli Bistro fusilli pasta
   Garlic & Parsley
2-1/2 cups fusilli pasta (Catelli)
1-1/2 cups white rice or basmati rice
chow mein noodles (optional)
pine nuts, pecans or walnuts (optional)

Other

aluminum foil (Alcan), reg & heavy duty

Spices

celery salt
chili flakes (optional)
curry powder
garlic powder
Mrs. Dash Italian Seasoning
Mrs. Dash Original Seasoning
poultry seasoning
salt & pepper

Baking Goods

brown sugar
canola oil
olive oil (optional)
vinegar

Helpers

chicken broth, 2 lge tetrapaks
   (60 oz or 1.8 L)
1 can sliced mushrooms (10 oz or 284 mL)
1 jar Catelli Garden Select pasta sauce
   Parmesan & Romano (24.5 oz or 700 mL)
BBQ sauce (or see back cover)
soy sauce (V-H)
Worcestershire sauce
oyster sauce
chili sauce, hot (bottled)
mayonnaise, lowest-fat
1/4 cup orange juice (McCain)

Frozen Food

4 cups peas & carrots blend
2 cups Oriental Style vegetables

Bakery

8-12 multigrain buns (2 recipes)

Custom Grocery List

Recipe Names   **Page #**

_____
_____
_____
_____
_____

Meats

Dairy

Produce

Dry Essentials

Spices

Baking Goods

Helpers

Frozen Food

Bakery

Other

Recipe Name	Page #
Szechuan Orange-Ginger Chicken	82
Beef Barley Soup	84
Hot Turkey Sandwiches	86
Spanish Patties	88
BBQ Chicken	90

Meats

real prepared bacon bits (optional)
lean ground beef 2-1/2 lbs or 1.125 kg
   (90% lean), 2 recipes
3 boneless skinless chicken breasts
   (1 lb or 450 g)
sliced deli turkey 3/4 lb or 350 g
   (or precooked roaster chicken)
8-12 boneless skinless chicken thighs
   (1-3/4 lbs or 800 g)

Dairy

1% milk
1 egg
butter or margarine (optional)

Produce

prepared garlic (in a jar)
2 onions
15 mushrooms
1 small red pepper
2 celery stalks
1 lge head green leaf lettuce
2 tomatoes
2 oranges

Dry Essentials

1-2 pkg mushroom or garden vegetable
   flavored rice (approx 6 oz or 165 g/pck)
cornflake crumbs (near coating mixes)
3/4 lb or 350 g vermicelli pasta (Catelli)
chow mein noodles (optional)
salted peanuts (optional)
1/4 cup pot barley
1 pkg dry poultry gravy mix, near spices
   (approx 1 oz or 30 g)

Bakery

6-8 slices whole wheat bread
croutons (optional)
4-6 whole wheat buns

Spices

bay leaf
cumin
ginger, ground
Mrs. Dash Italian Seasoning
Mrs. Dash Original Seasoning
onion flakes
parsley, dried
rosemary (not ground)
salt & pepper

Baking Goods

canola oil
cooking spray (PAM)
olive oil, extra-virgin
baking powder
cornmeal
flour
brown sugar
white sugar

Helpers

BBQ sauce (or see back cover)
hot ketchup
ketchup (optional - for fries)
chunky salsa
chili sauce, hot (bottled)
dry-garlic sauce (V-H)
tahini (ground sesame seeds, looks like
   peanut butter)
1/2 cup beef broth
1 can tomato soup (10 oz or 284 mL)
1 can consomme (10 oz or 284 mL)
1 can diced tomatoes (14 oz or 398 mL)
1/2 cup orange juice (McCain)
poppyseed dressing (or see back cover)
black olives (optional)

Frozen Food

4 cups broccoli
2 cups baby carrots
2 cups baby peas
5 minute fries (McCain SuperQuick)
   (1 lb or 450 g)

Other

aluminum foil (Alcan), reg & heavy duty
1/4 cup sherry (or red wine)

We Include
4 Types of Indexes
for Speed

Main Component

chicken, beef, etc.
'cause you have an idea
of what you'd like

Color

for the times when
speed is everything

Alphabetical Listing

'cause you remember
the name

Fat Content

from lowest to highest
'cause your health requires you
to watch your fat intake

I
N
D
E
X

Index by Main Component

Beef

Chicken

Pork

Index by Main Component

Vegetarian

Index by Color (Cont.)

Index by Alphabetical Listing

Index by Fat Content

From Kitchens Across The Country

I saw Sandi on Canada A.M. just by chance one day and even though skeptical (another cookbook?) bought her book. I always meant to get organized myself with our own limited menu plan. The amount of work and organization in this book is mind boggling. Everyone now seems to have an interest in the week ahead and I have more help and participation than ever before!

Janet Dean   Cape Breton Nova Scotia

I had the opportunity to meet Sandi at a book signing in Ottawa. I was inspired to buy the book and decided to put it to the test when having friends over. We had lavish stuffed chicken with roasted potatoes and veggies. It was a hit as are the others we've done since. The recipes are easy and the ingredients are basic. Thank you for publishing this book!

Judy Durocher   Kingston Ontario

Our family is in week eight of your cookbook, Life's on Fire - Cooking for the Rushed and I am already dreading when we run out of weeks! I thank you for writing a cookbook that has improved my life for the first time ever!

Shannon Gilbert   St-Lazare Quebec

Tasty nutritious supper every night!! I also have to say, I'm saving money on food. No more am I tossing out food that I bought for a recipe I'll never make!

Jan Krysko   Edmonton Alberta

I just had to write and rave about your cookbook. I've bought dozens of cookbooks, even the rushed kind, and still always manage to burn supper! You hold my hand and assume I can't do anything, which I can't! Thank you, Thank you, Thank you!!!

Monica Shearer   Beeton Ontario

120

...about Life's on Fire

The result of your work is changing my life for the better. I want to thank you again and again and again, not only for myself but for the other working mothers that will now have a better quality of life too! God Bless!

Helene Leblanc   Deux-Montagnes Quebec

What an awesome book!! These recipes are great, grocery bill down…nutrition, variety and ease up! My family gives every recipe a rating of either 9 or 10 out of 10. This book is unlike any other cookbook I have seen.

Judy Buchynski   Edmonton Alberta

I read a positive review about your book in a Winnipeg community newspaper. I took it out from the library and became addicted to using it after two short weeks. I finally ordered myself a copy. I want to thank you for your extraordinary cookbook!

Pauline Rey-Rivard   Winnipeg Manitoba

We are now in the ninth week of your fabulous book. It has changed our lives. My son who is 12 makes a lot of the meals himself. My daughter recently commented that's it's neat that we now eat when it's still light outside! Here's to my lifesaver - Sandi.

Christina Bertolissio   Windsor Ontario

This cookbook is more than just recipes - it's an attitude and a lifestyle! Everyone who has a life needs this book!

Mary Defeo   Nelson British Columbia

Sandi's cookbook has changed our lives! It has simplified our grocery shopping, significantly reduced our shopping costs, filled our lives with great tasting, easy-to-prepare meals (that are good for you) and… I now love cooking!

Tanja McCallum   Guelph Ontario

Thank you! Thank you! Thank you!

"I only clean my house spotlessly, for people I don't care for."

I would not clean my house for the following people...

For our dear, dear **friends** who have hung in there through thick and thin. The last 1 1/2 years have been "On Fire" to say the least. Our time may have been spread thin between Ron and I, kids and work, but a day doesn't go by without you in our hearts!...Thanks for always saying the right things and letting us know we're in your hearts too. Gee we pick good friends!!!

Gerry and Rick...what can I say, what would we have done without you? Your kindness and time will never ever be forgotten!

To our beautiful neighbors **Bill and Betty** who had to put up with our messy yard while our home was being built. In return for our mess, you would smile, have kind words, and then mow our lawn! Lucky us!

To our **test families**. Thanks for your honesty! Without you, our books would not be as successful as they are!

To the **Hole's**. You are the most amazing group of down to earth people I've ever been blessed to know (Ok, Bruce, I know you're not officially a part of the family...but we love you too!) Thank you for always lending a hand when we're not sure!!!

A very warm and heartfelt thanks to **Elite Lithographers**...the best of the best...I think that says it all!

Also to Jim and the gang at **Friesens**. Thanks for coming along for the ride!

To my beautiful brother **Bruce** and his wife (my friend) **Jane**. Thank you so much for your love and support when I needed it more than you may know!

Last but not least to my beautiful mother in law, Solange (**Mom**). Your positive attitude and your shining eyes have been so important when things got a little crazy. Thanks for believing and making us feel like it was normal that we ask you to give up your time...on demand! We love you so much!

Thanks to the following stores and their **great staff** for helping us add that **special touch** to our photographs.

Le Gnome (the most fantastic kitchen shop with all the perfect accessories).
Tierra Sol Ceramic Tile (for the most amazing selection of tiles).
Above the Bank Interiors (for the best selection in Kravet and other fabrics).
Touchwood Flooring (the only place to buy hardwood flooring in Alberta).
Hole's (a gardener's ultimate destination).

HOLE'S
Enjoy Gardening

Emile Henry
Poterie culinaire
FRANCE

A special thanks to
Browne & Company
for supplying all the dishes
in the photographs.

available
across Canada at
fine kitchen stores
and The Bay

122

Ron Richard

Ron was on the cover of Life's on Fire, so he didn't get his mug in the back. He's the guy at the helm…the guy who runs a well greased machine! Being the project manager of Cooking for the Rushed doesn't always put Ron in the lime light, but there's no doubt…without him there would not be any books!….Bonus…I just happen to be in love with him!!!

Ian Grant

Ian has been with us forever…right Ian? He has been through it all. When I approached Ian for the first book, he was one of the few photographers who saw taking photos that were not food styled as a challenge. Ian is such a pleasure to work with. Once again, there are just not enough thank yous. Ian Grant Photography Inc. is located in St. Albert, Alberta.

Tannie Cyr

The graphic arts designer from heaven! Tannie takes her work to heart and is always there to put out our little fires. At the tail end of publishing, every little thing that can go wrong, does. She just smiles and says her famous…"No Problem!" Tannie is the owner of "It's your Thing Design" in Edmonton.

Lorna Bennett

Once again Lorna pulls off my warped sense of humor! When I explained how I wanted the cover to look, she made me slump my shoulders, make that "I'm too hot and frustrated" face and took a picture! She's given me her word that picture will never been seen in public! Thanks again, Lorna!
Lorna is the owner of Lorna Bennett Illustration in Edmonton.

From the Author!

I may moan while I eat...but I met my match! When I met Ron, I couldn't believe someone had the same passion for food as I did! We are like two excited kids every time we step into a restaurant (which isn't often). We sit side by side and open up the menu...but when the waiter arrives we ask the infamous question... "What do people come here for?" After a little prodding they spill the beans! "We'll have one of those, and one of those!" Let the sharing begin!!!

Eating has always been a passion of mine, however, I never liked weekday cooking, until I turned it into my hobby. It was not until then that I began to get excited about finding out yet another new way to cut down my prep times for the workweek, while perfecting flavors. I never saw it as my fulltime career. I had my job...and then there was my hobby, food! I couldn't wait to learn more.

Ron knew that I wanted to help people with weekday cooking and to improve their lives, like I had improved my own eating life! I had the food vision and he never doubted for a minute I could spread the word and make a difference! I guess you could say, he just saw the big picture. Since we began, it's hard to tell who gets more excited about a new e-mail from yet another person whose life has changed. Oooor about trying some new recipe or some new flavor. Now that we know how much you love and trust our food...There's just no stopping us!

Wishing you all many moans over dinner!

Sandi Copeman-Richard

Canadian Order Form

Order 2 - 9 items (any combination) for 20% off　　**(Single item price in brackets)**

"Getting Ya Through the Summer" ($19.99) NOW $15.99 x _____ = _____

"Life's On Fire" ($29.99) NOW $23.99 x _____ = _____

"Life's On Fire" (Butt Proof) Apron ($39.99) NOW $31.99 x _____ = _____

Order 10 items or more (any combination) for 25% off

"Getting Ya Through the Summer" ($19.99) NOW $14.99 x _____ = _____

"Life's On Fire" ($29.99) NOW $22.49 x _____ = _____

"Life's On Fire" (Butt Proof) Apron ($39.99) NOW $29.99 x _____ = _____

Shipping: $4.90 for 1 - 4 items _____
Order 5 or more items for free shipping*
(Applies only if mailed to same address in Canada)

Cooking for the Rushed Inc.

SUBTOTAL _____

Add 7% GST + _____
Subtotal x 0.07 = GST

TOTAL AMOUNT _____
(Prices quoted are in Canadian Dollars)

Payment:　❏ **Visa**　❏ **Mastercard -** order by mail, fax or online
❏ **money order** (shipped immediately)
❏ **cheque** (allow 2 - 4 weeks)

Payable to: Cooking for the Rushed Inc.
Box 2056, Cochrane, Alberta, Canada T4C 1B8
Phone: (403) 851-1268, Fax: (403) 851-1266
Toll Free: 1 (866) 551-1268

SHIPPING INFORMATION: (Please Print)

Name _____

Address _____

City _____　**Province** _____

Postal Code _____　**Phone (_____)** _____

E-mail _____　**Fax (_____)** _____
Please include city/area code

CREDIT CARD INFORMATION

Order online at **www.cookingfortherushed.com** for quickest delivery time.

Name (as on Credit Card) _____

Credit Card Number _____ _____ _____ _____

Expiration Date __ __ / __ __ **(month/year)**

Signature _____

United States Order Form

Order 2 - 9 items (any combination) for 20% off   <u>(Single item price in brackets)</u>

"Getting Ya Through the Summer" ($13.99) NOW $11.19 x _____ = _____

"Life's On Fire" ($20.99) NOW $16.79 x _____ = _____

"Life's On Fire" (Butt Proof) Apron ($27.99) NOW $22.39 x _____ = _____

Order 10 items or more (any combination) for 25% off

"Getting Ya Through the Summer" ($13.99) NOW $10.49 x _____ = _____

"Life's On Fire" ($20.99) NOW $15.74 x _____ = _____

"Life's On Fire" (Butt Proof) Apron ($27.99) NOW $20.99 x _____ = _____

Shipping: **$5.90 for 1 item, $1.00* for each additional item** + _____
Order 14 or more items for free shipping*
*(Applies only if mailed to same address in United States)

**Cooking
for the
Rushed
Inc.**

TOTAL AMOUNT _____
(Prices quoted are in U.S. Dollars)

Payment: ❑ **Visa**   ❑ **Mastercard -** order by mail, fax or online
❑ **money order** (shipped immediately)
❑ **cheque** (allow 6 - 10 weeks)

**Payable to: Cooking for the Rushed Inc.
Box 2056, Cochrane, Alberta, Canada T4C 1B8
Phone: (403) 851-1268, Fax: (403) 851-1266
Toll Free: 1 (866) 551-1268**

SHIPPING INFORMATION: (Please Print)

Name _____

Address _____

City _____ **State** _____

Zip Code _____ **Phone (_____)** _____

E-mail _____ **Fax (_____)** _____
Please include city/area code

CREDIT CARD INFORMATION - Credit card orders are billed in equivalent Canadian
dollars. The exchange rate will affect the final $US charge by your credit card company.
Order online at **www.cookingfortherushed.com** for quickest delivery time.

Name (as on Credit Card) _____

Credit Card Number _____ _____ _____ _____

Expiration Date ___ ___ / ___ ___ **(month/year)**

Signature _____

Check Us Out!

www.cookingfortherushed.com

National Bestseller

- ✔ Order Books Online
- ✔ Upcoming Events Schedule
- ✔ Published Articles
- ✔ Meal Planning Advice
- ✔ New Recipes
- ✔ Blank Grocery Lists
- ✔ Prepared Grocery Lists
- ✔ Product Information
- ✔ Fundraising Opportunities Available for Nonprofit Organizations

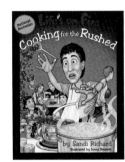

Coming Soon

• **Create your own customized printable grocery lists on our website**

• **"The Ultimate Meal Planning Kit - Cooking for the Rushed"**

• **"Whining and Dining - Cooking for the Rushed"**

Cooking
for the
Rushed
Inc.

Phone: (403) 851-1268 (Calgary & Area)

Toll Free: 1 (866) 551-1268

Fax: (403) 851-1266

We welcome any comments or suggestions.
Contact us by E-mail: rsrichard@cookingfortherushed.com

Life's on Fire
Cooking for the Rushed

What do you need?

... delicious tasting food?
... supper fast?
... food everyone will eat?
... to reduce mealtime stress?
... healthy balanced meals?
... to save money?
... easy to follow recipes?
... help in the kitchen?

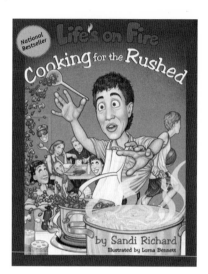

Helping thousands of families meal plan.

- Life's On Fire is the first book in the Cooking for the Rushed Series
- Life's On Fire has changed the supper dynamics for thousands of families across the country
- This book is as much about stress reduction as it is about creating delicious, quick suppers
- A meal planning guide teaching you to customize using your own recipes
- 12 weeks of amazing suppers with accompanying grocery lists
- Recommended by dieticians, nutritionists, nurses and doctors for healthy eating

Why Cooking for the Rushed books are your most valuable cookbooks

- tested and tested and tested by real families on the go
- each recipe is color coded for speed
- grocery lists accompany groups of 5 amazing suppers
- instructions for the entire meal
- easy to follow instructions next to each ingredient
- symbols identify meal component for ease of substitution
- photos of real food the way it looks when you prepare it
- specifically designed to reduce mealtime stress
- fast preparation times
- healthy balanced diet including a wide variety of cuisine
- detailed equipment lists
- nutritional data including diabetic food choices